Butterflies

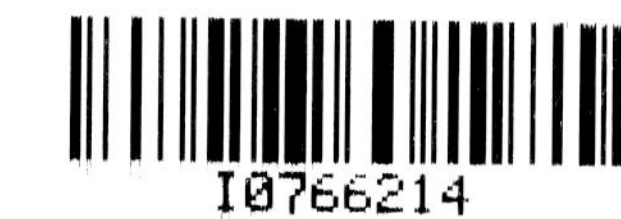

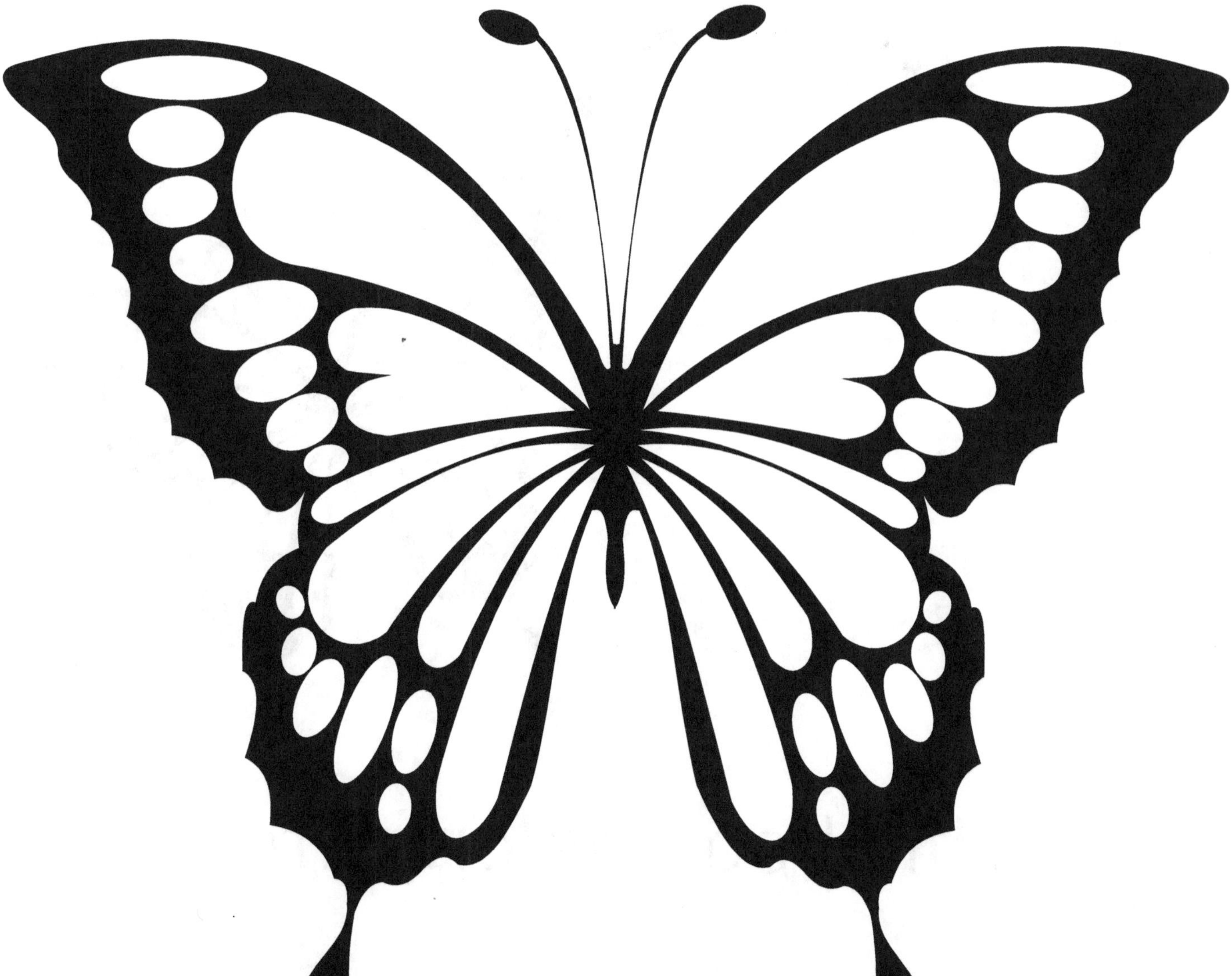

Coloring Book

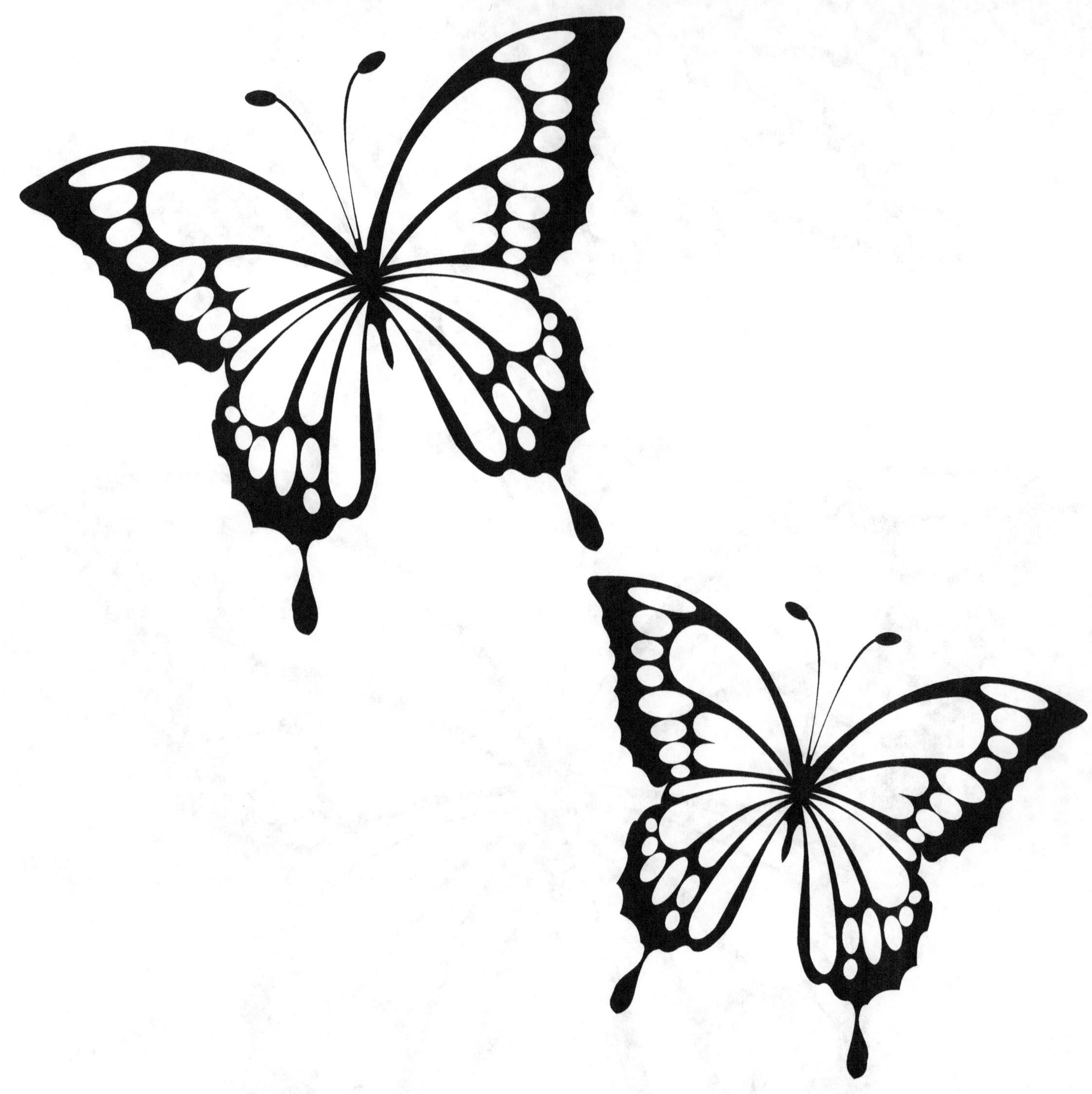

This book belongs to:

____

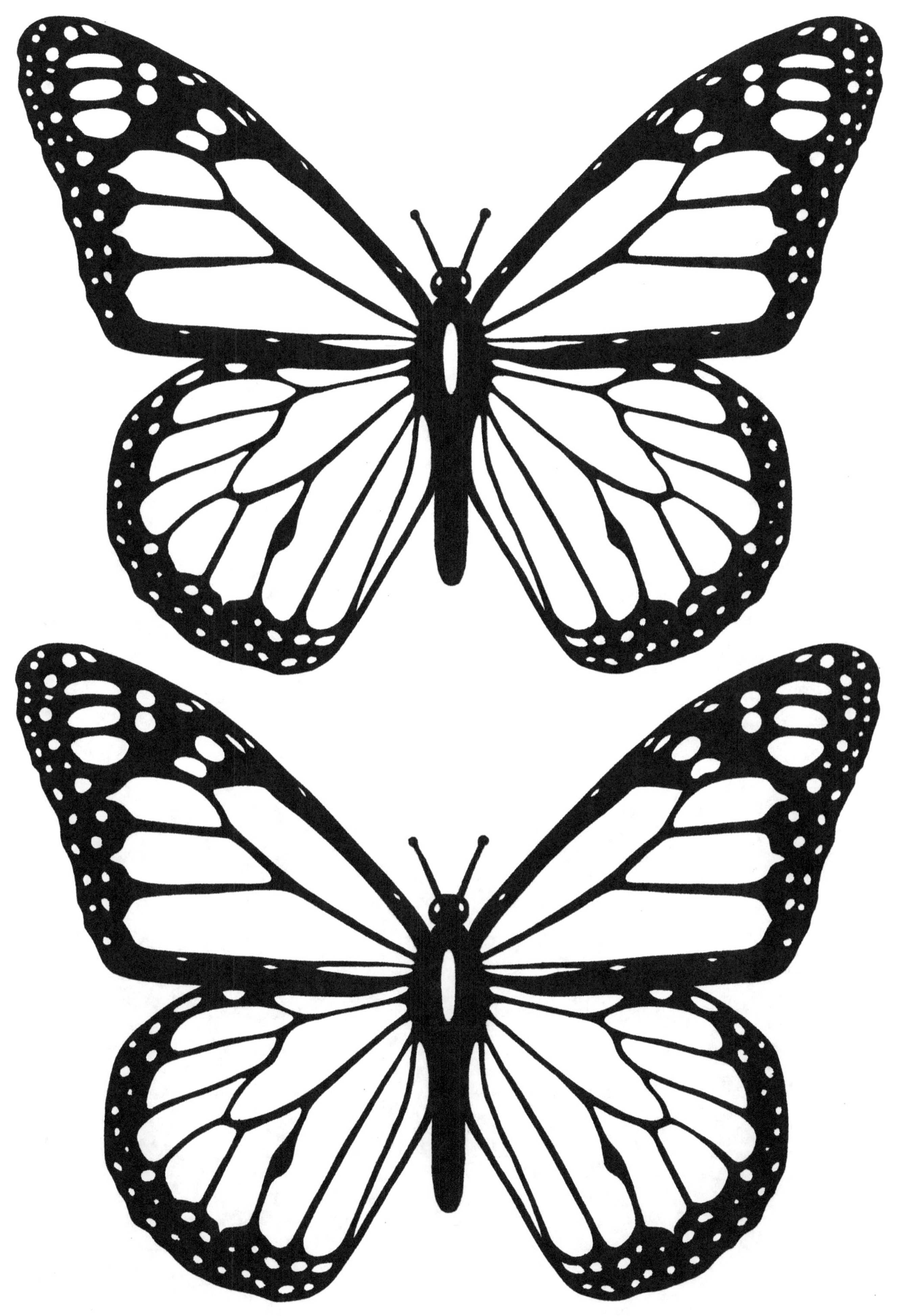

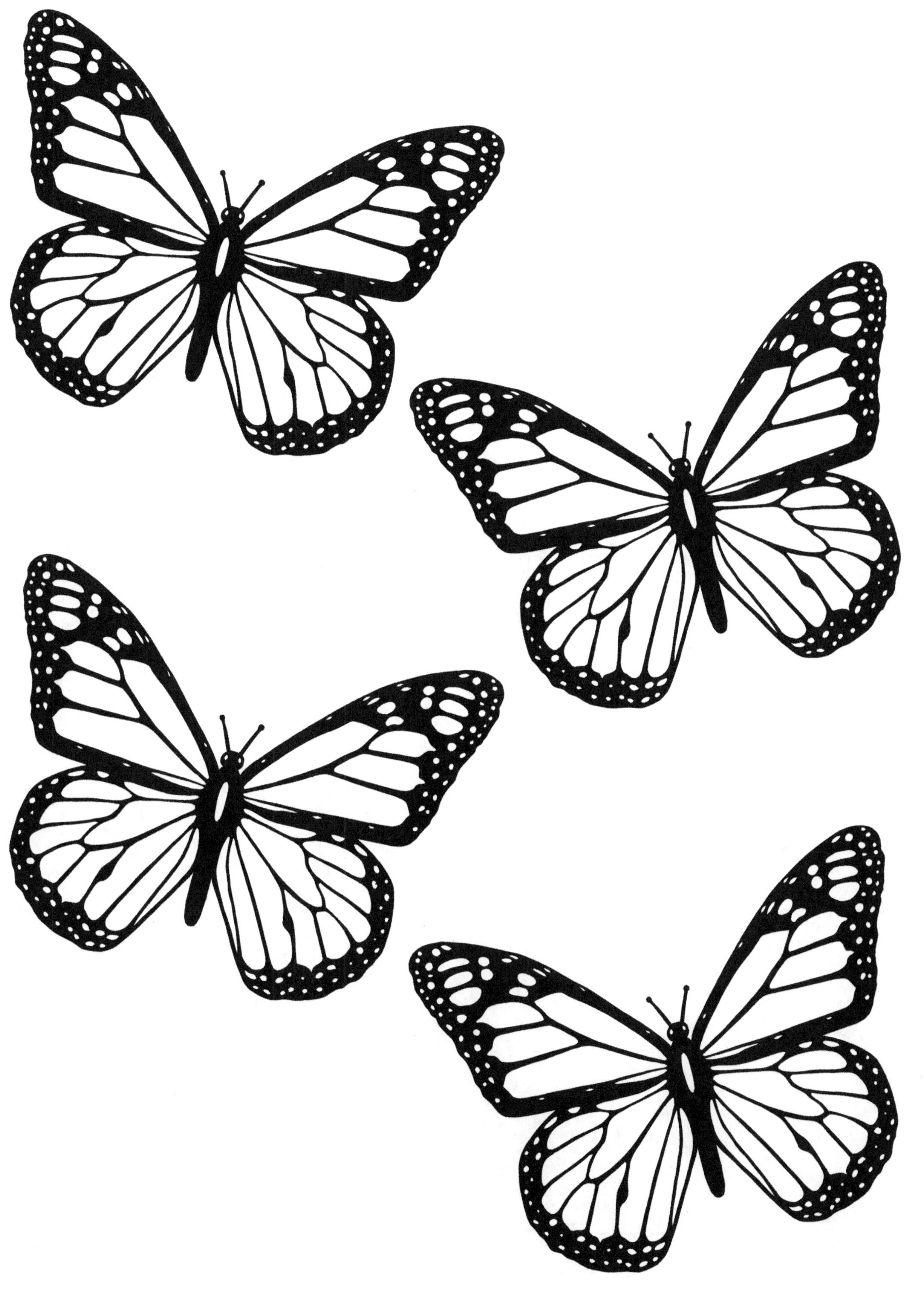

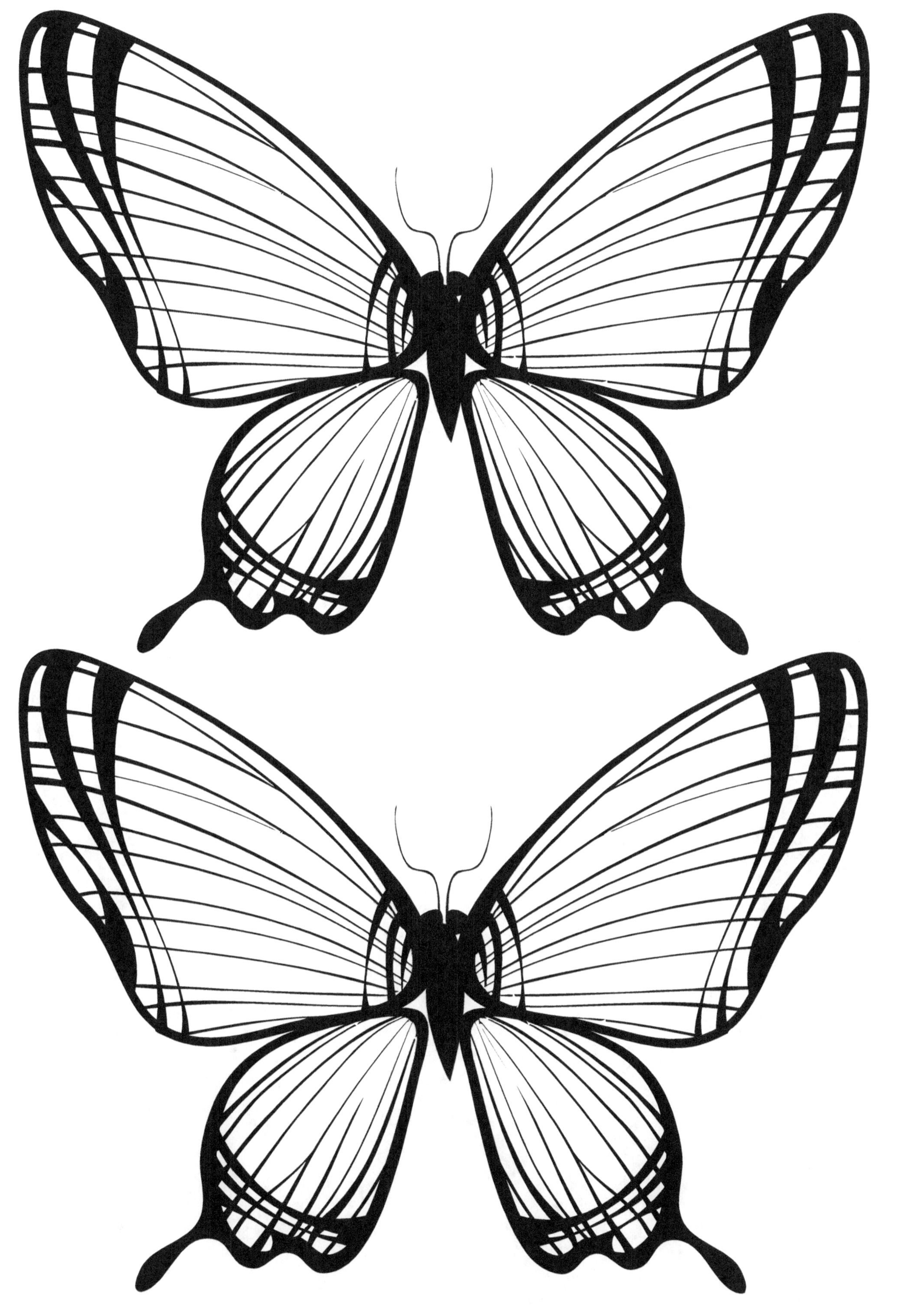

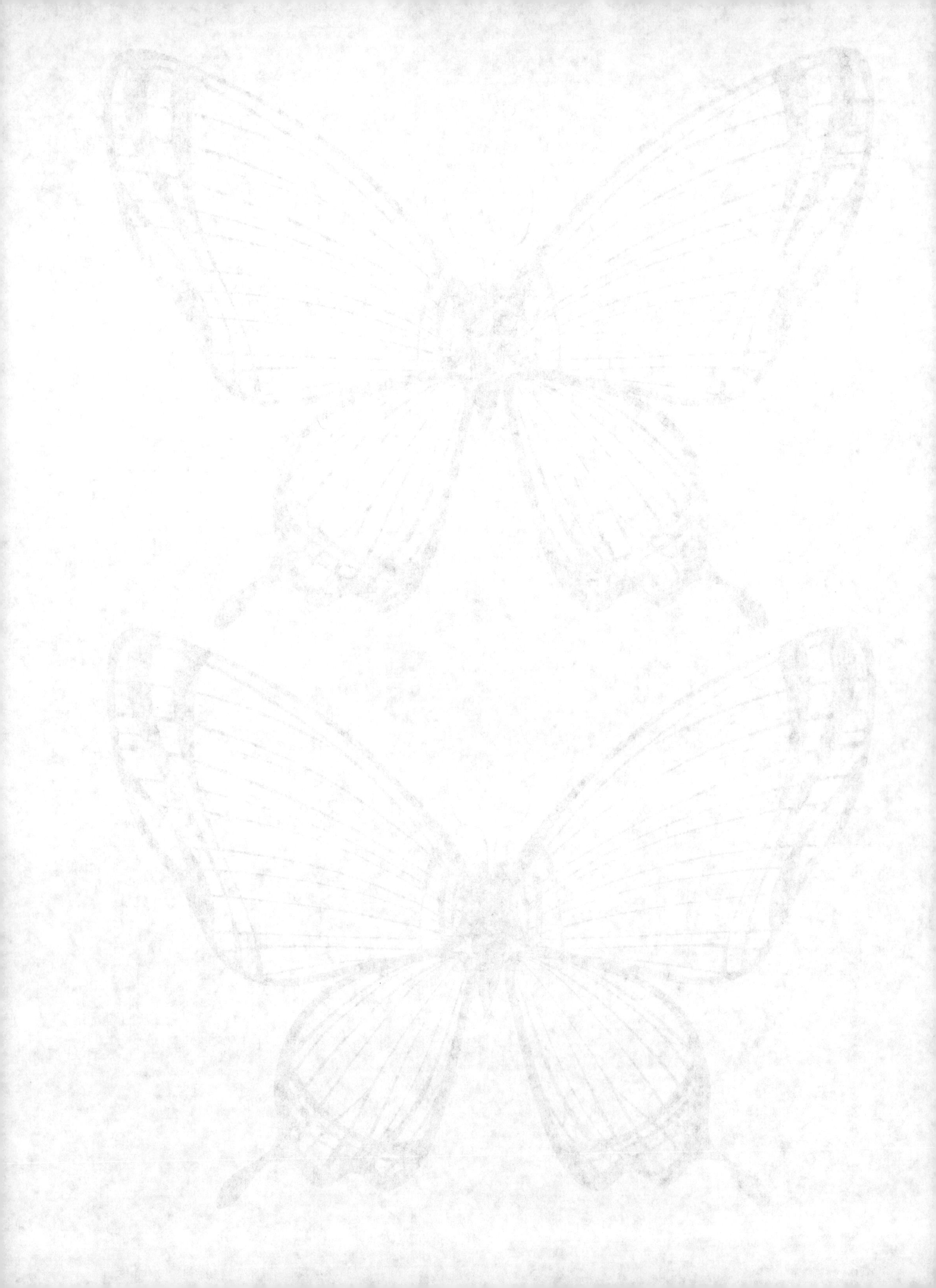

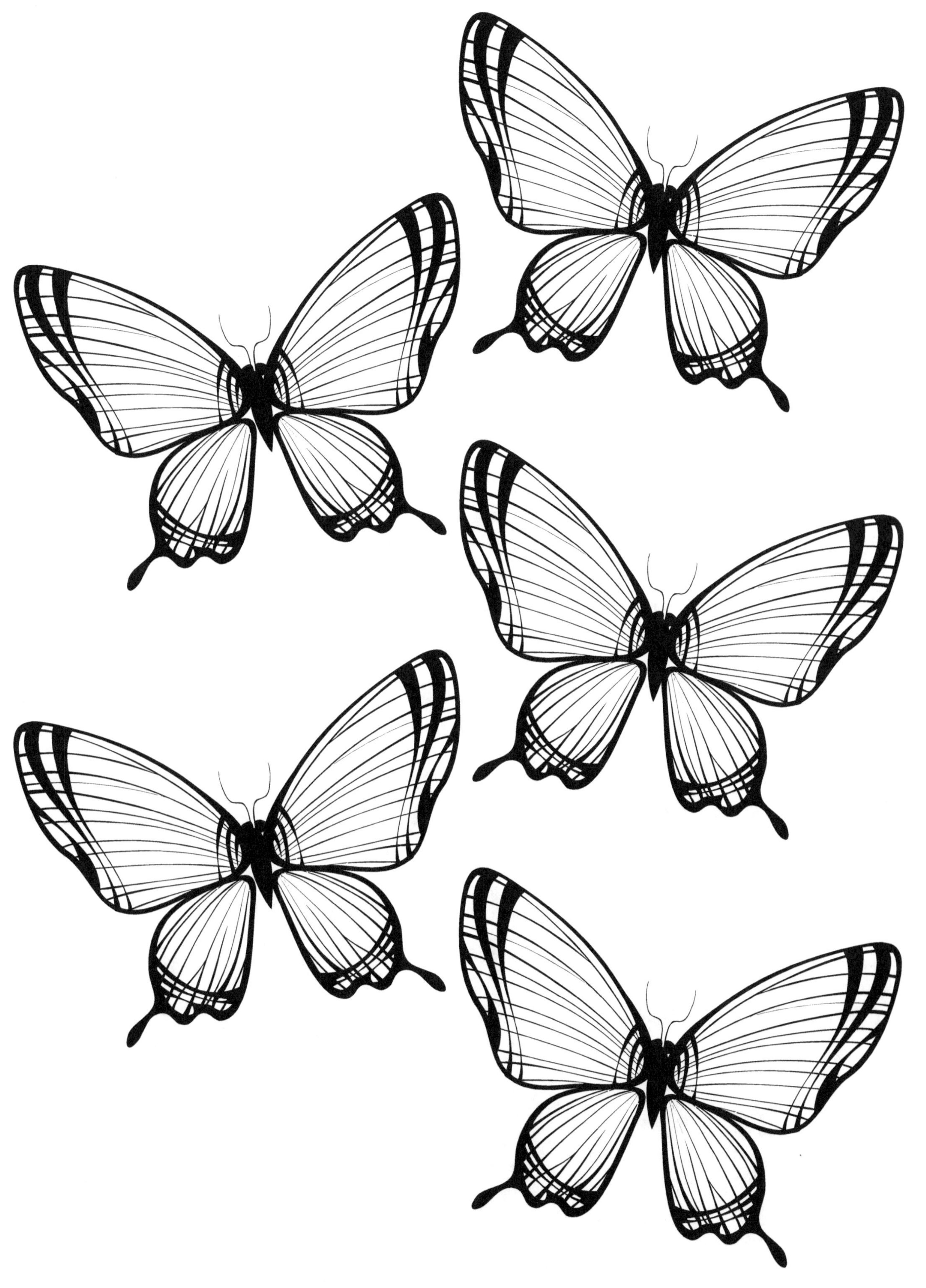

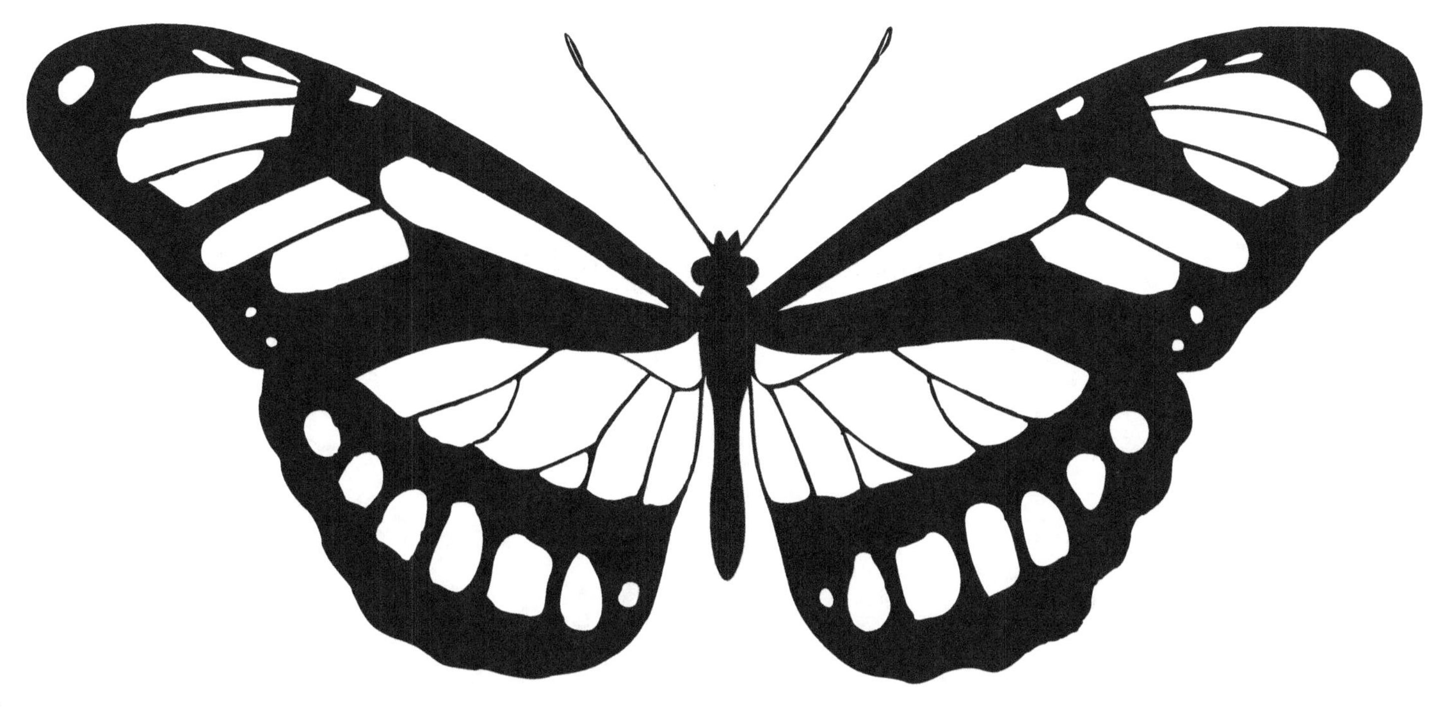

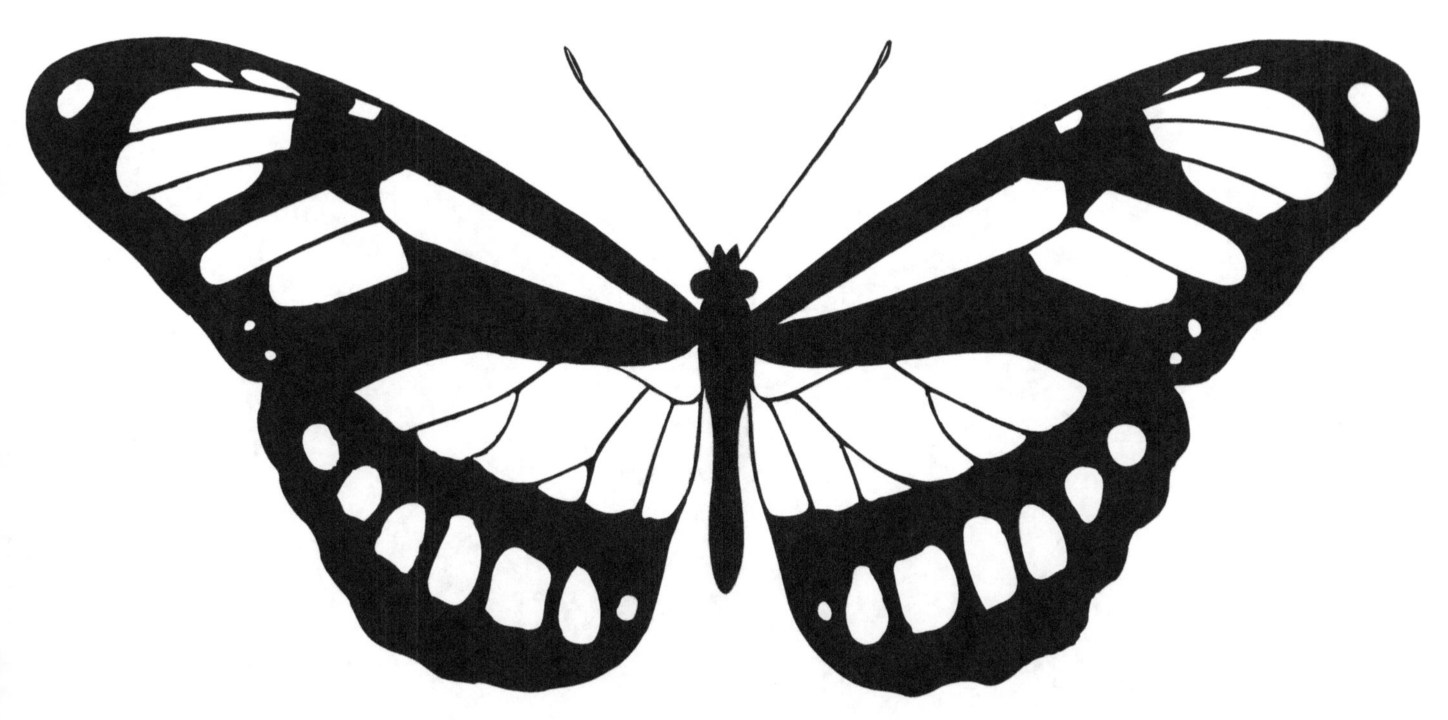

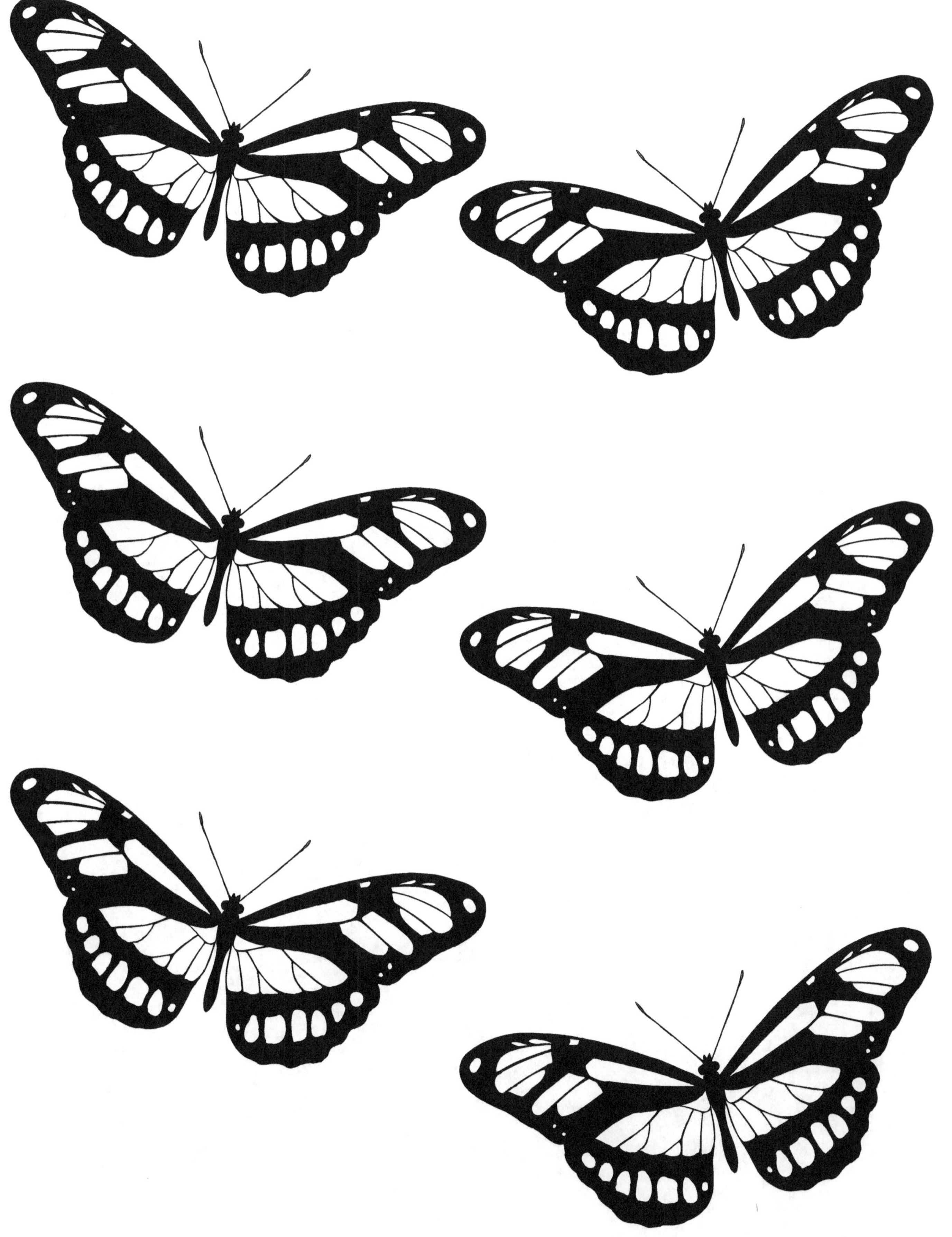

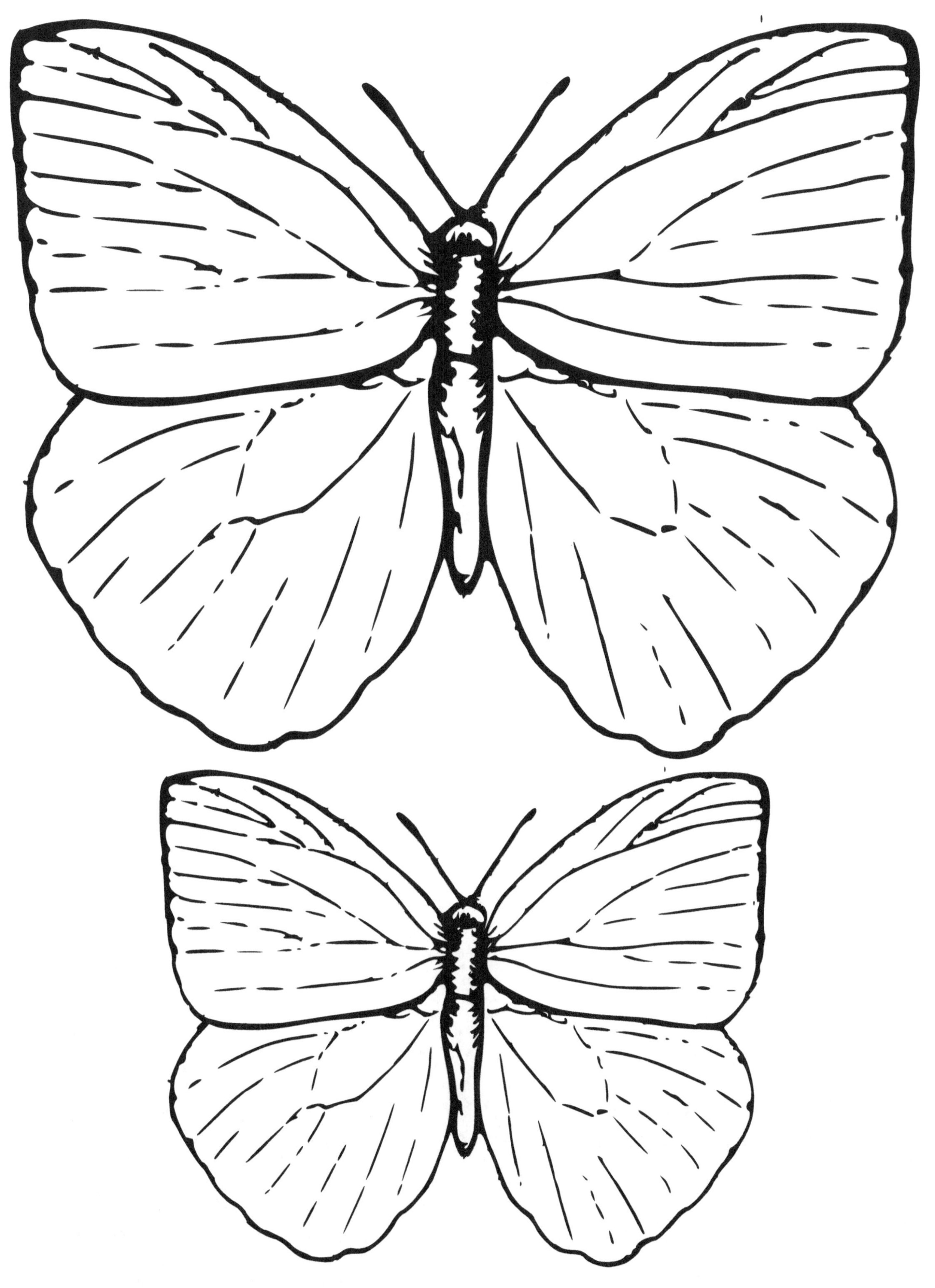

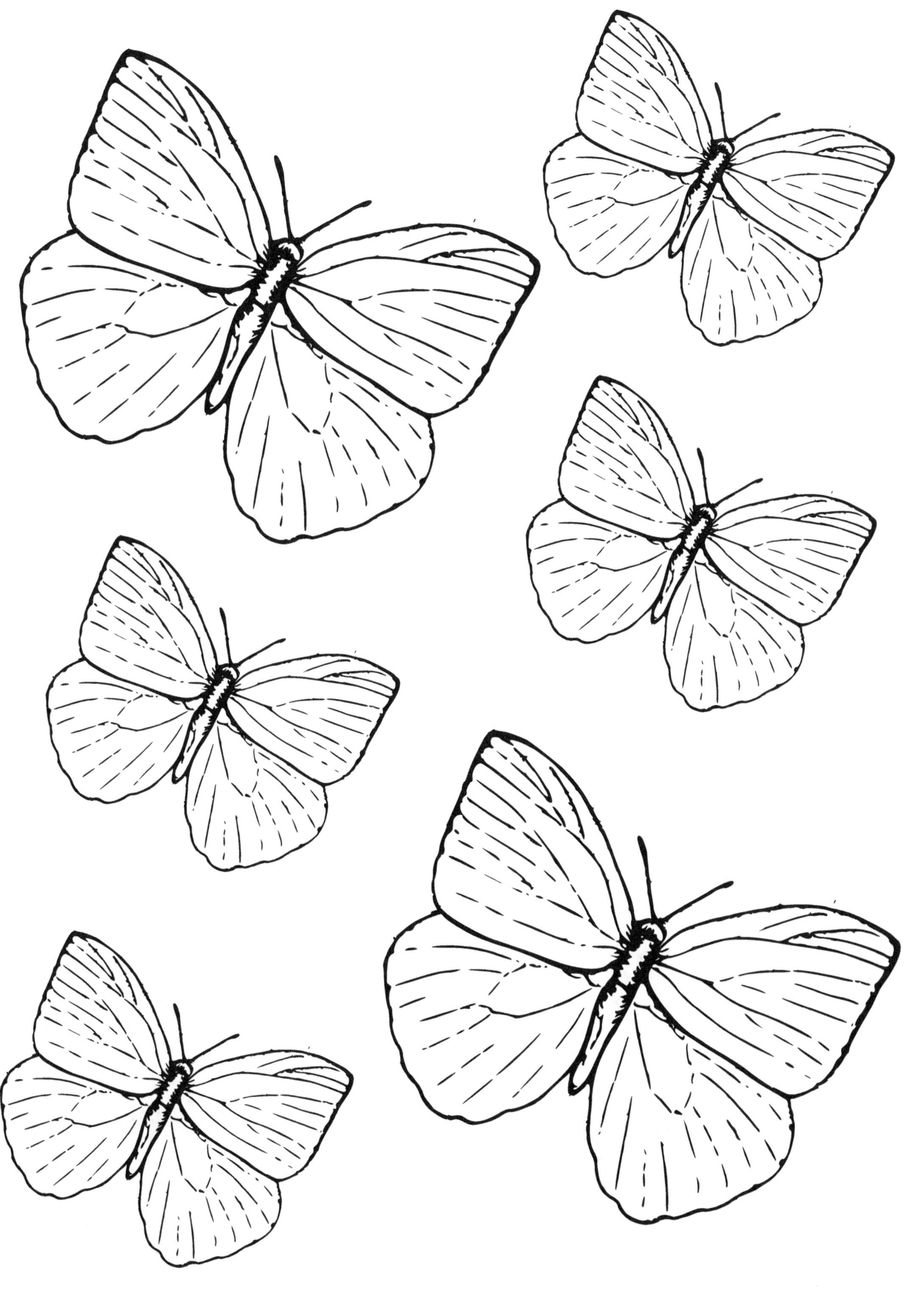

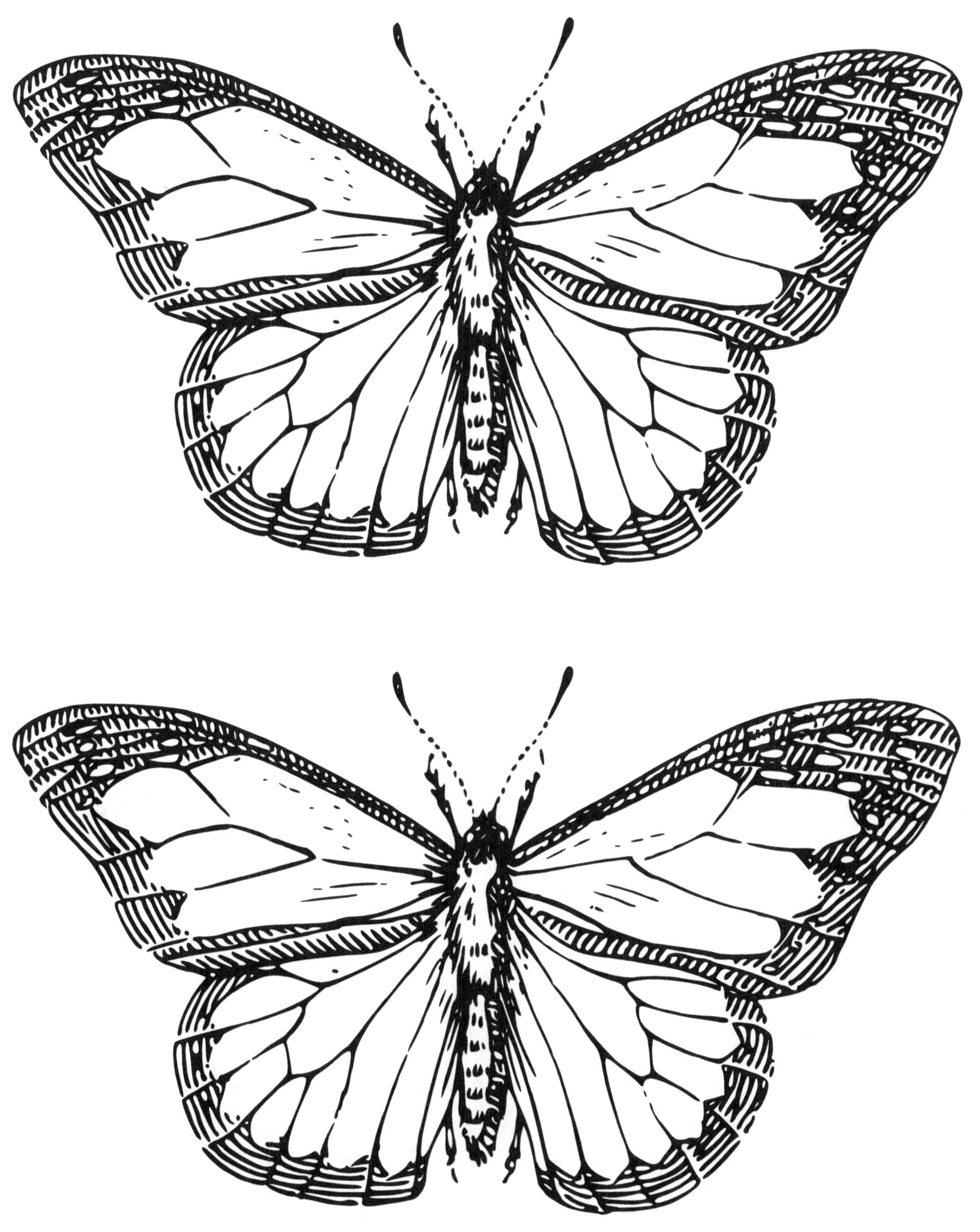

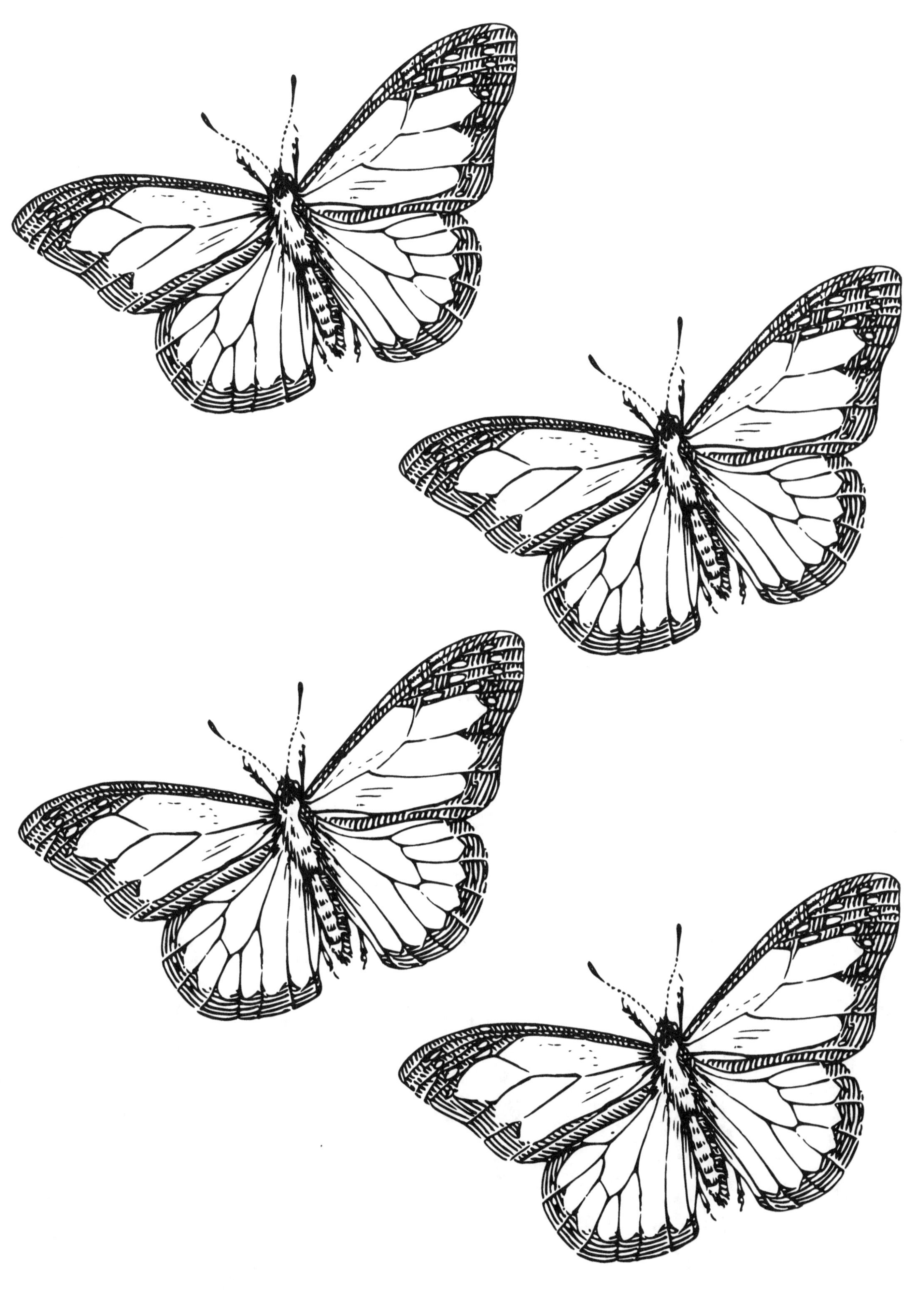

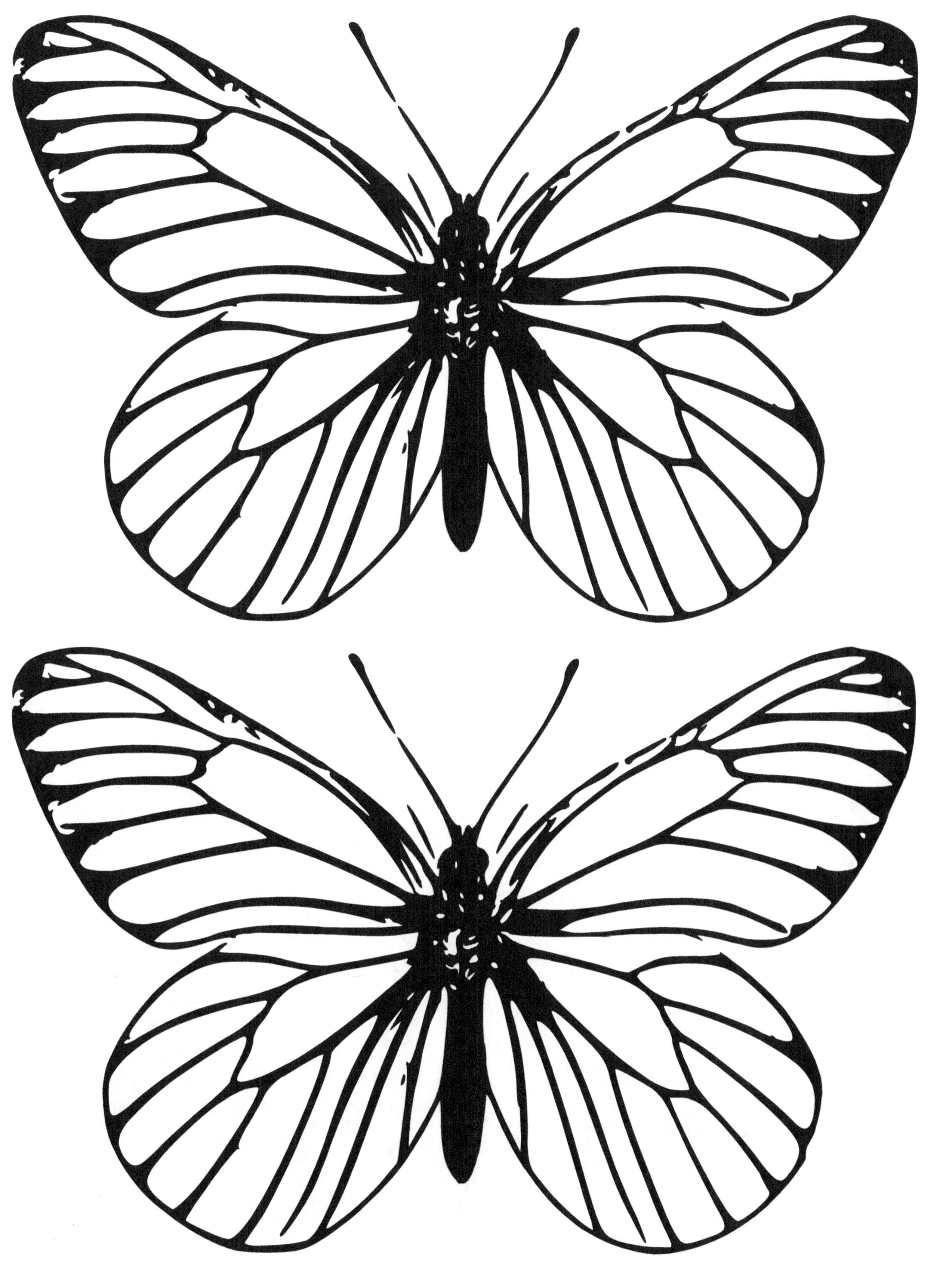

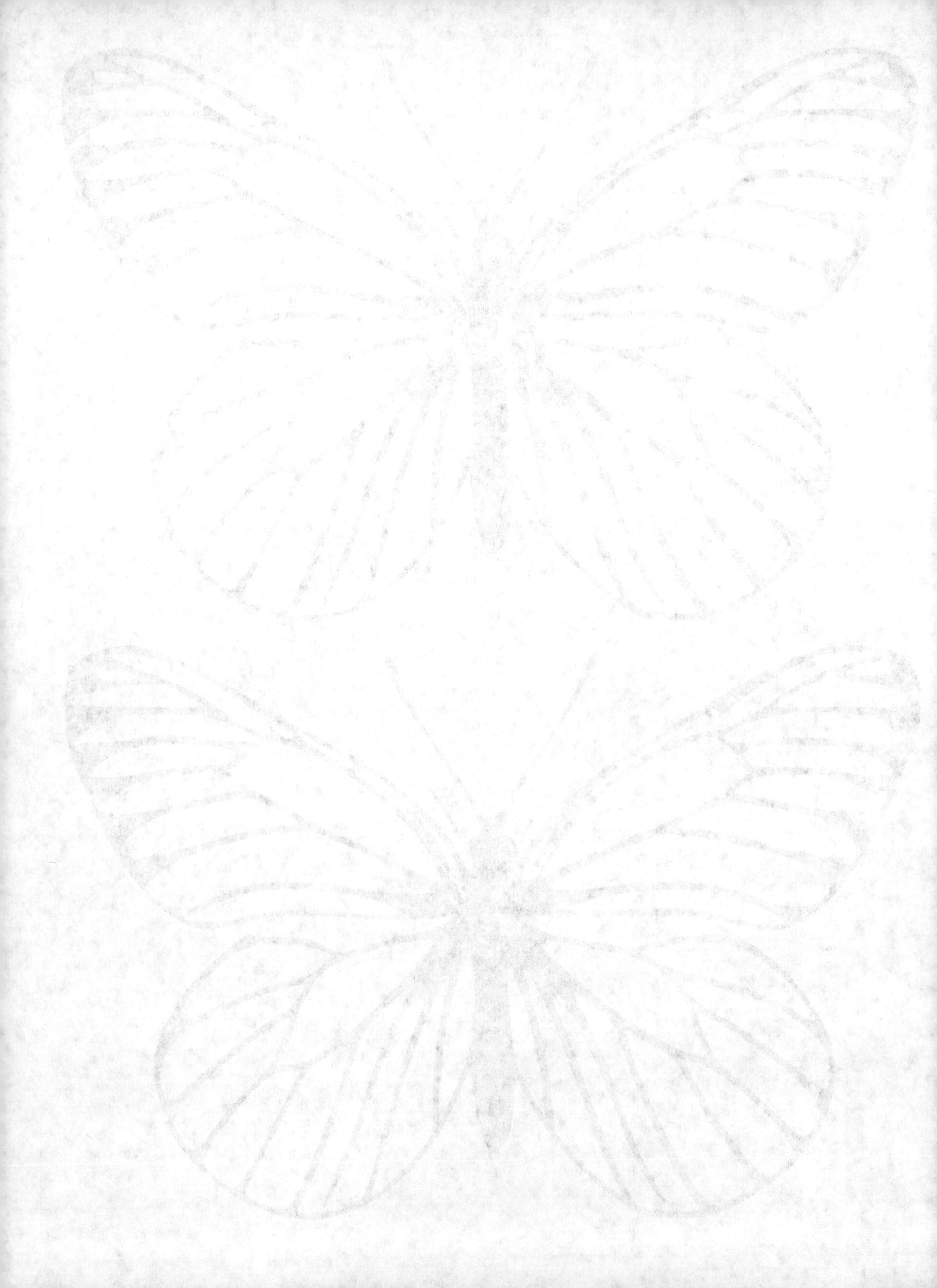

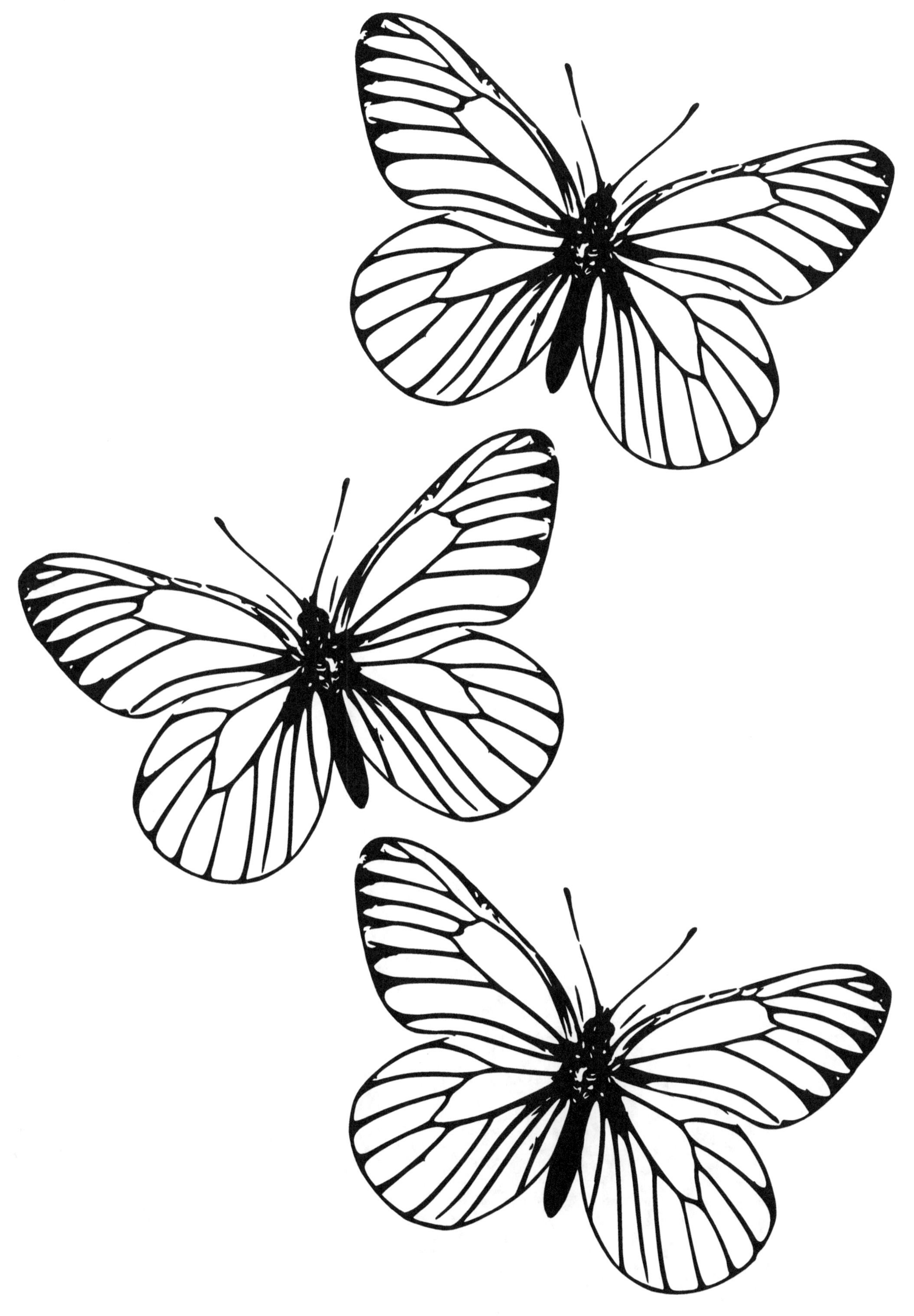

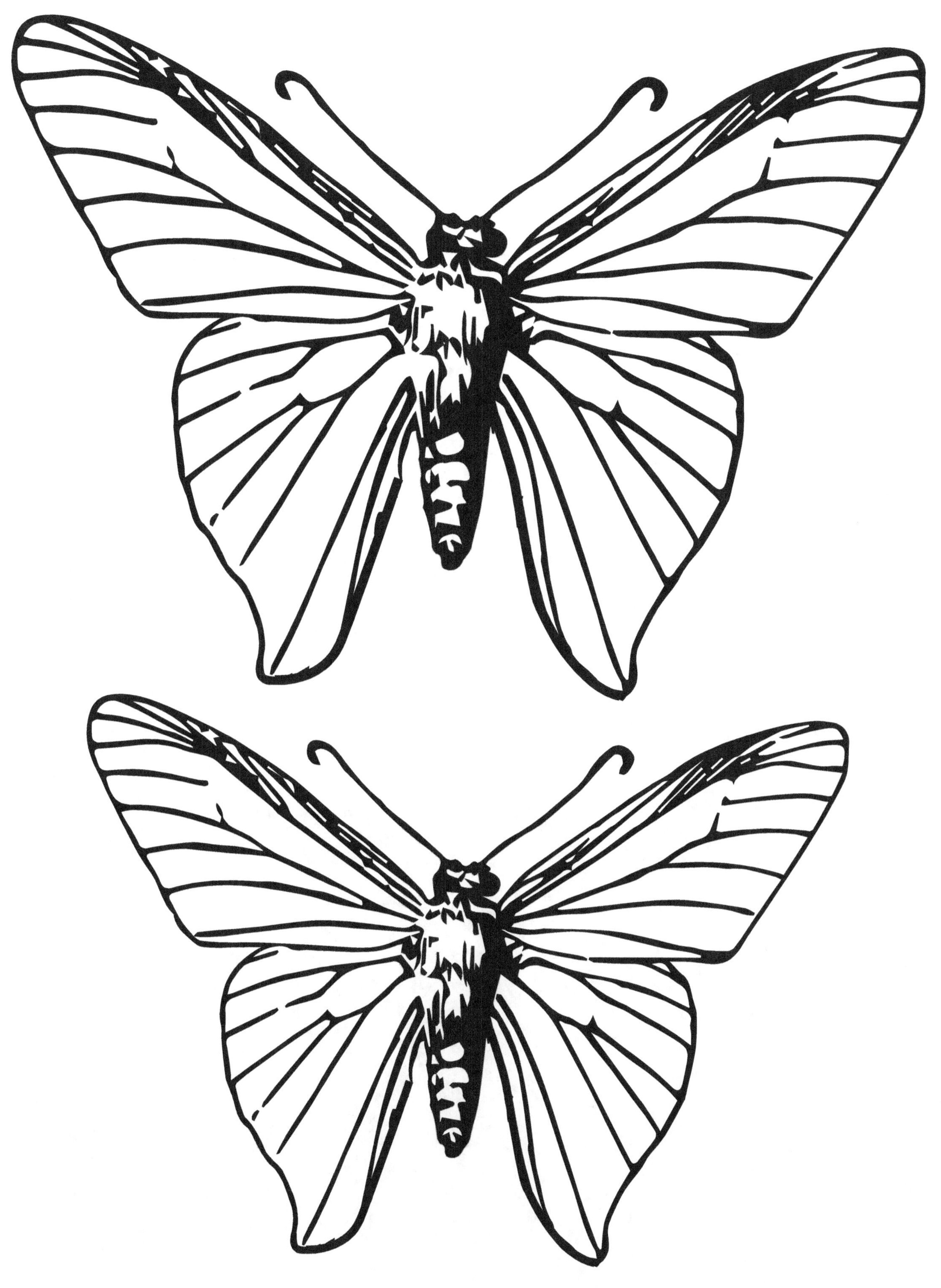

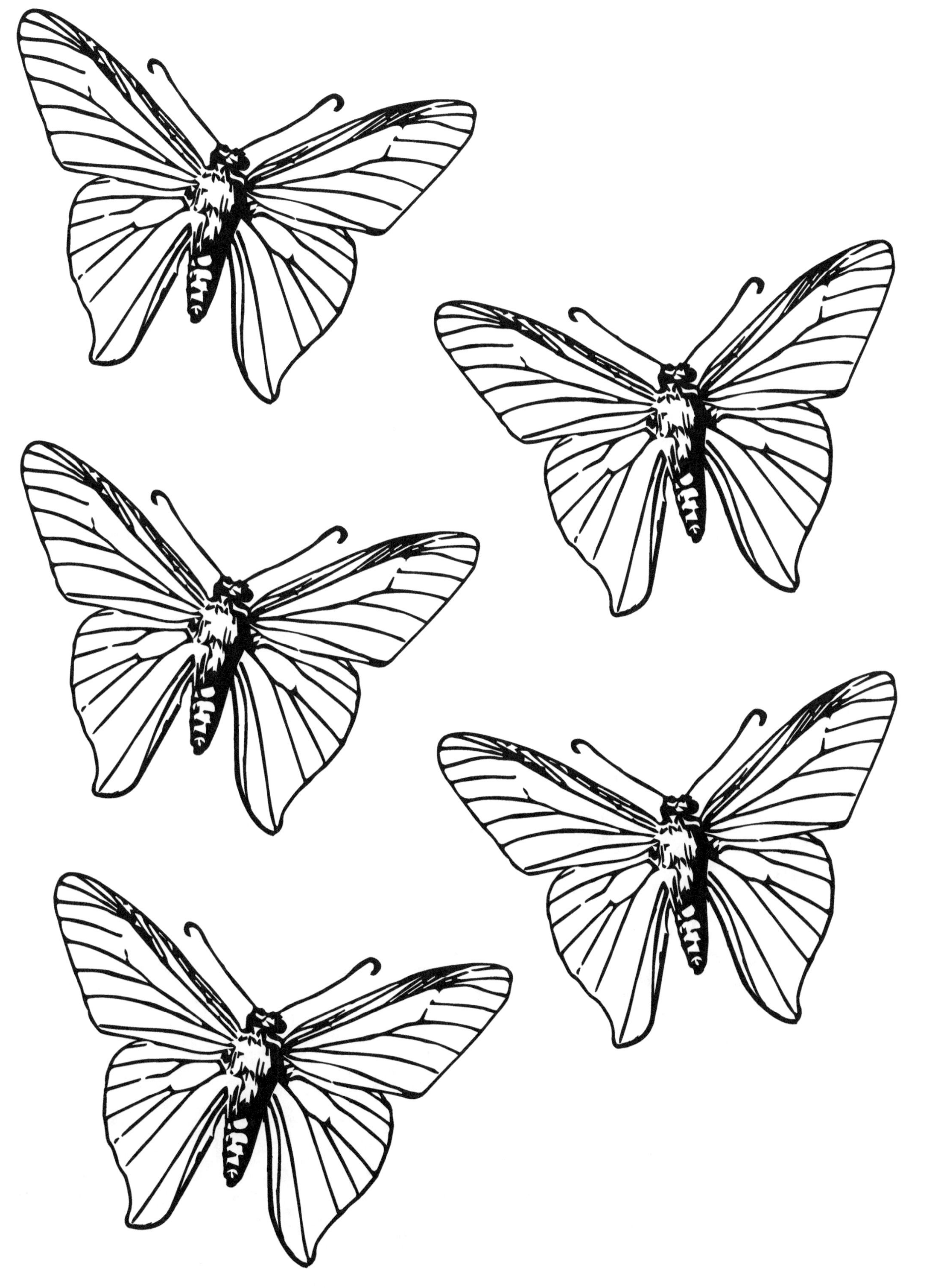

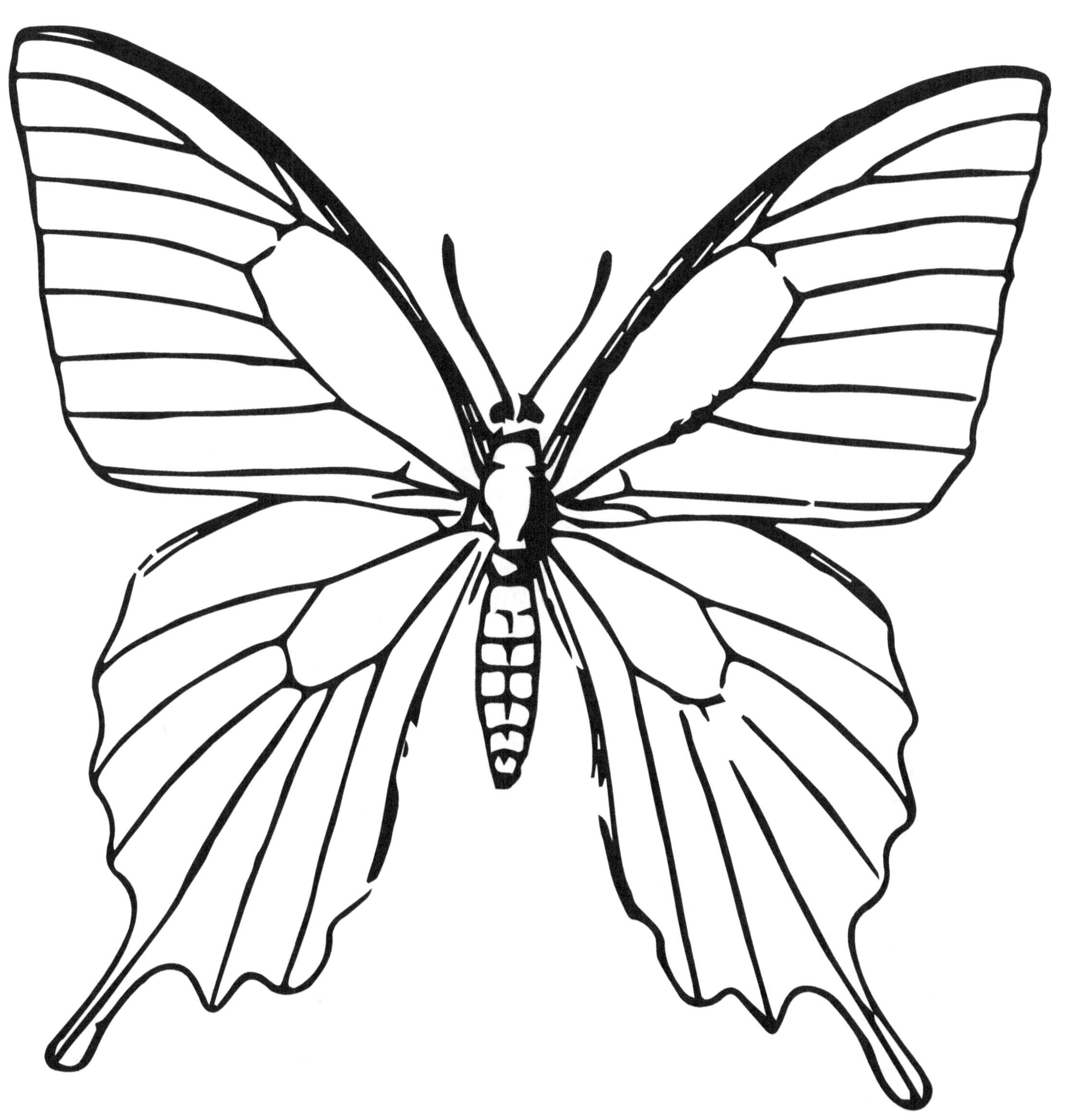

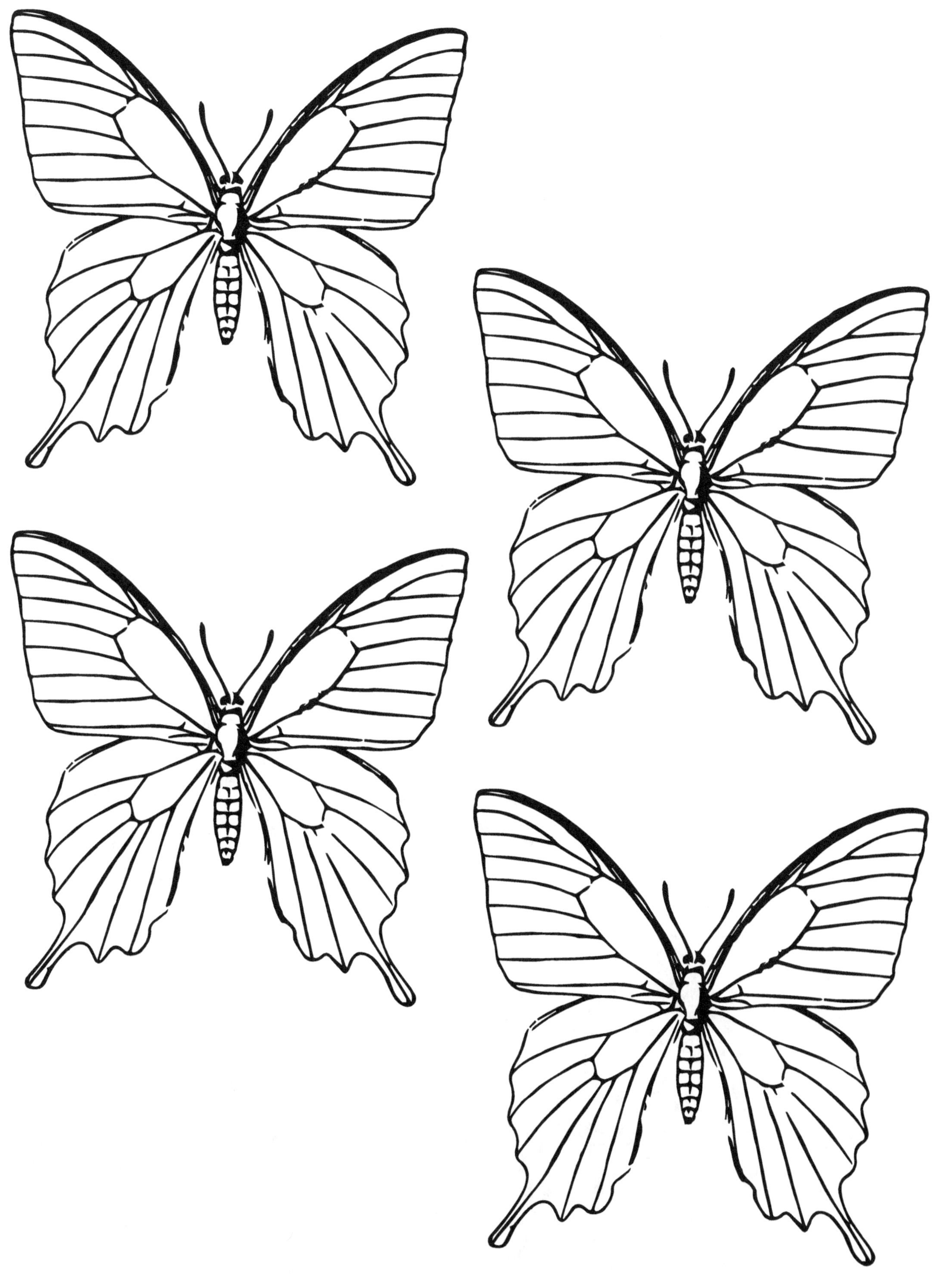

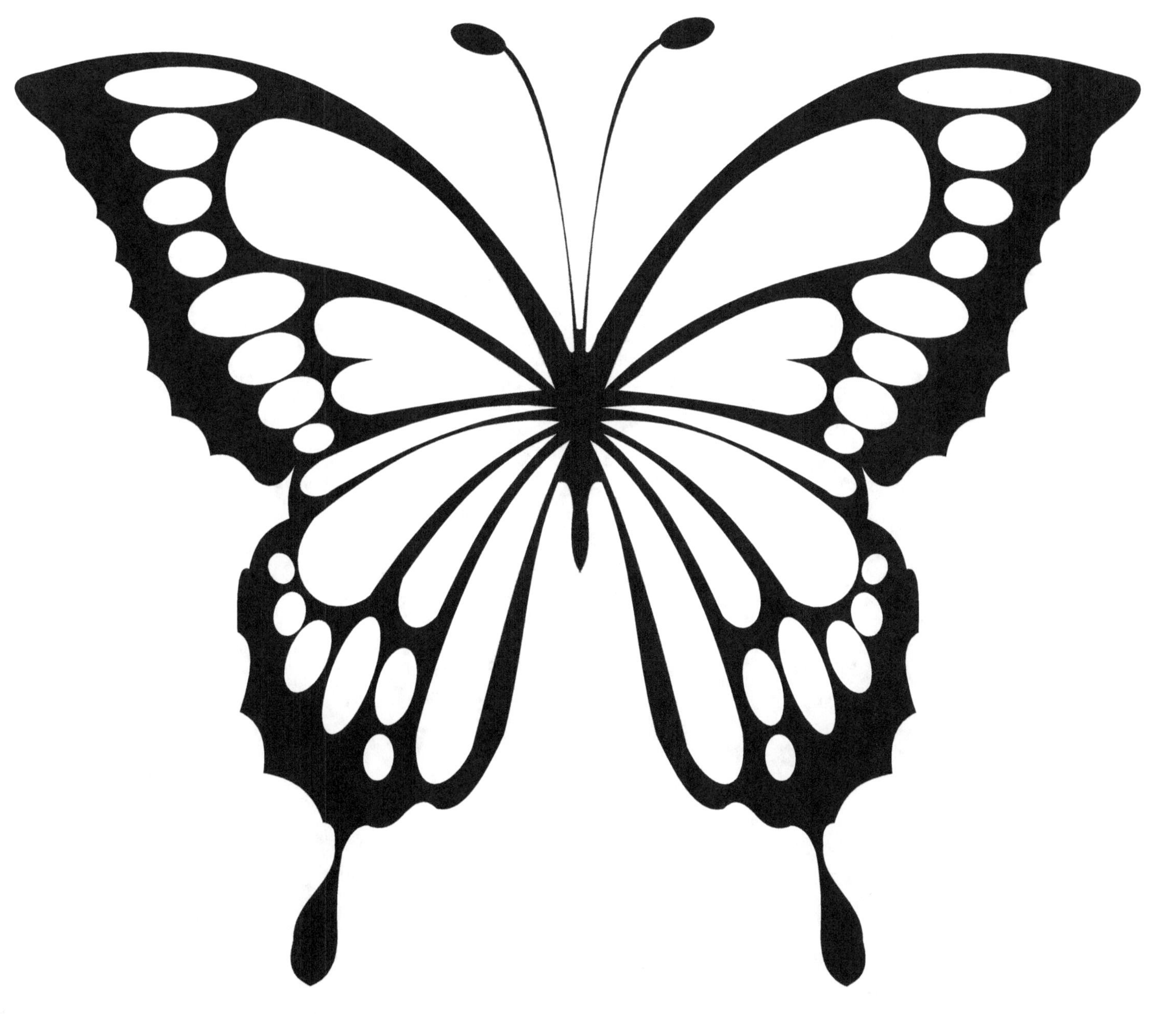

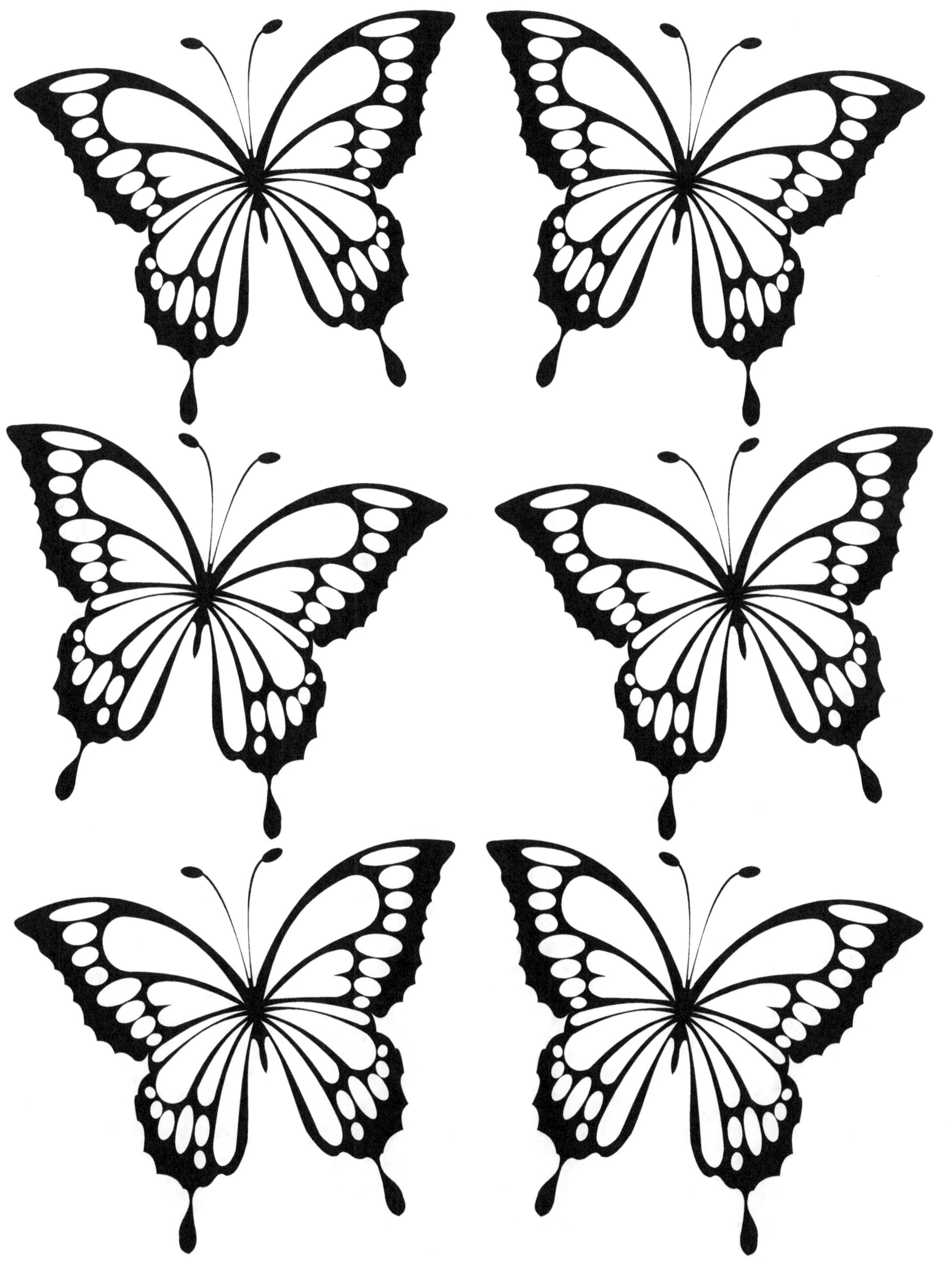

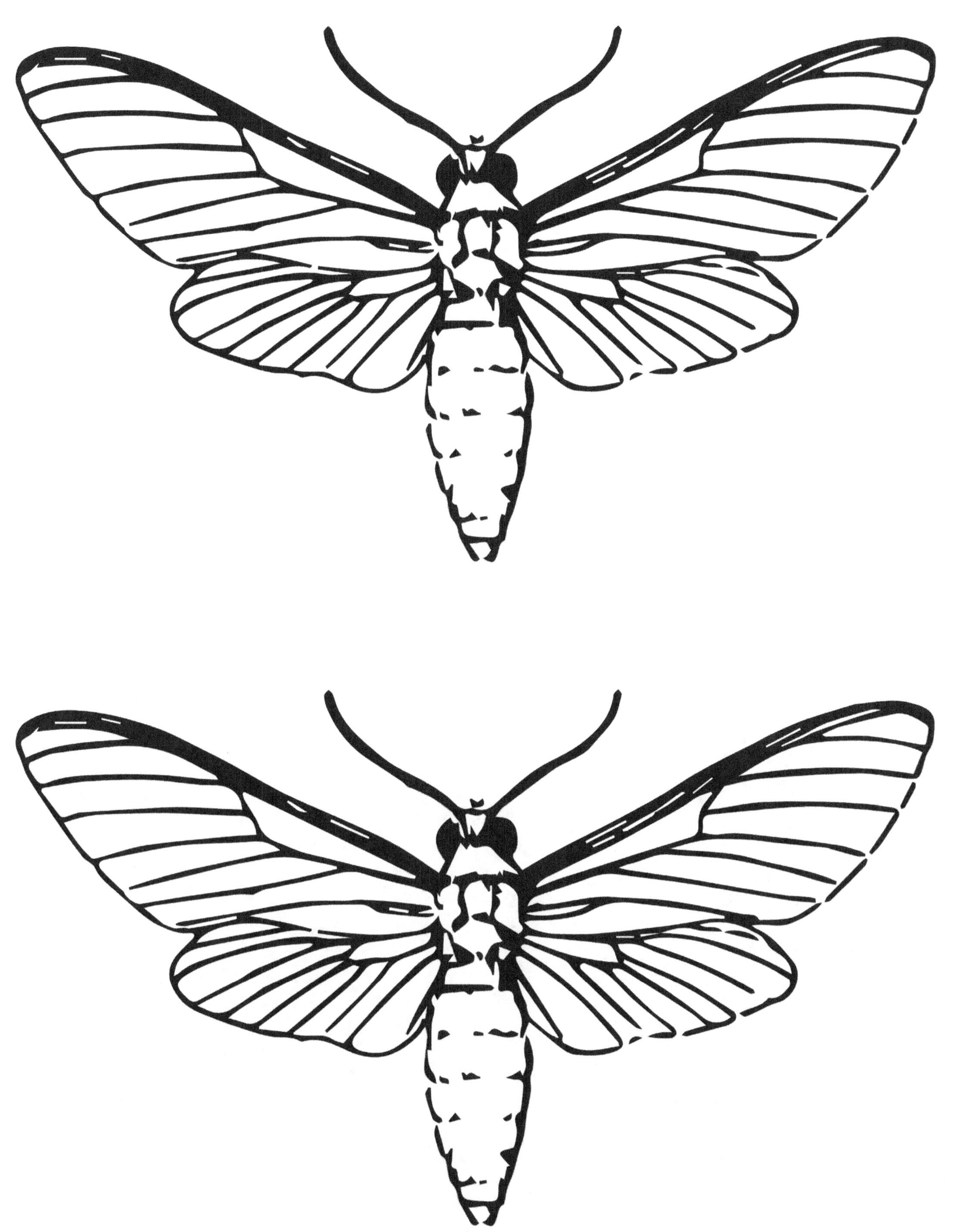

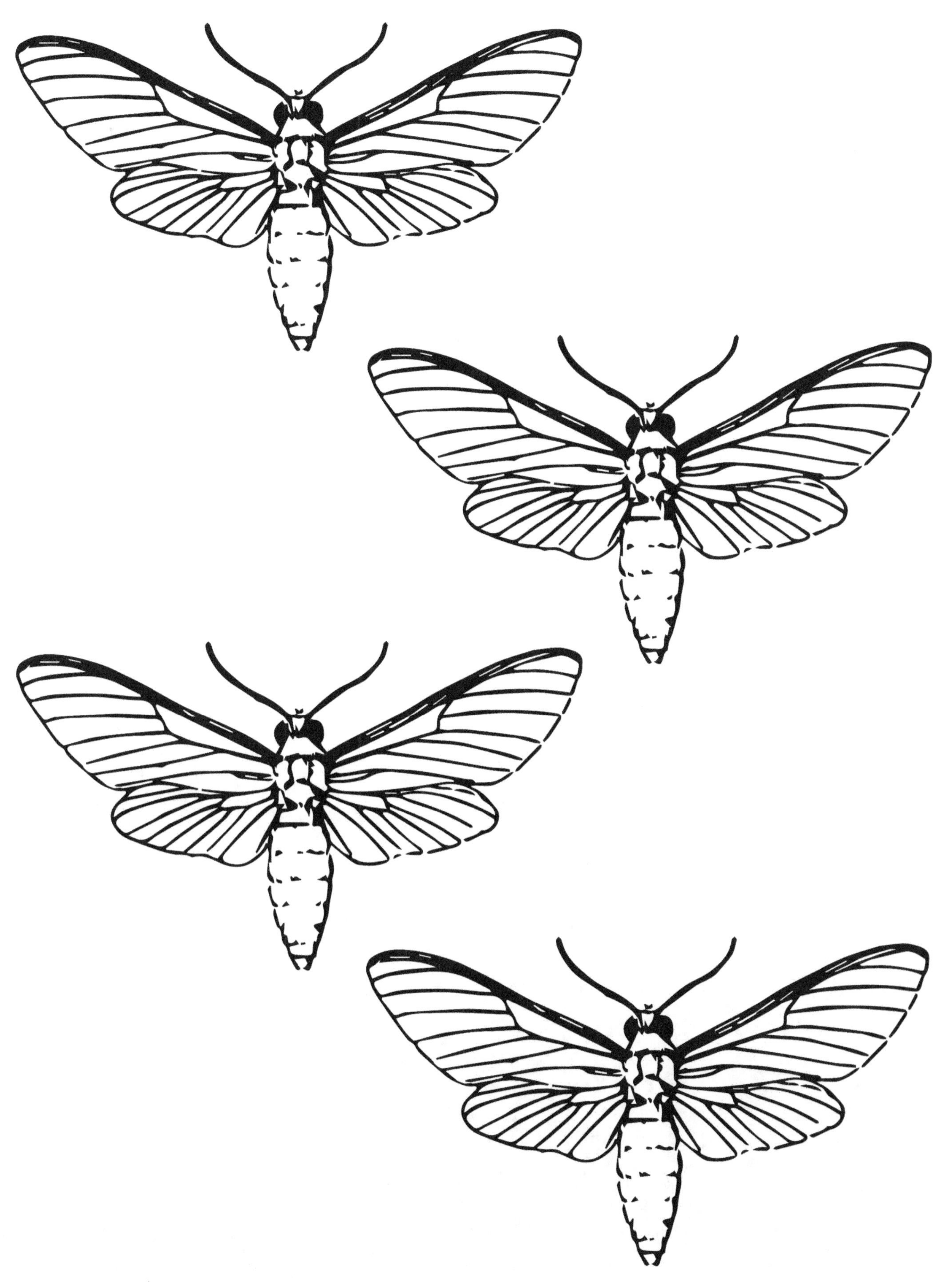

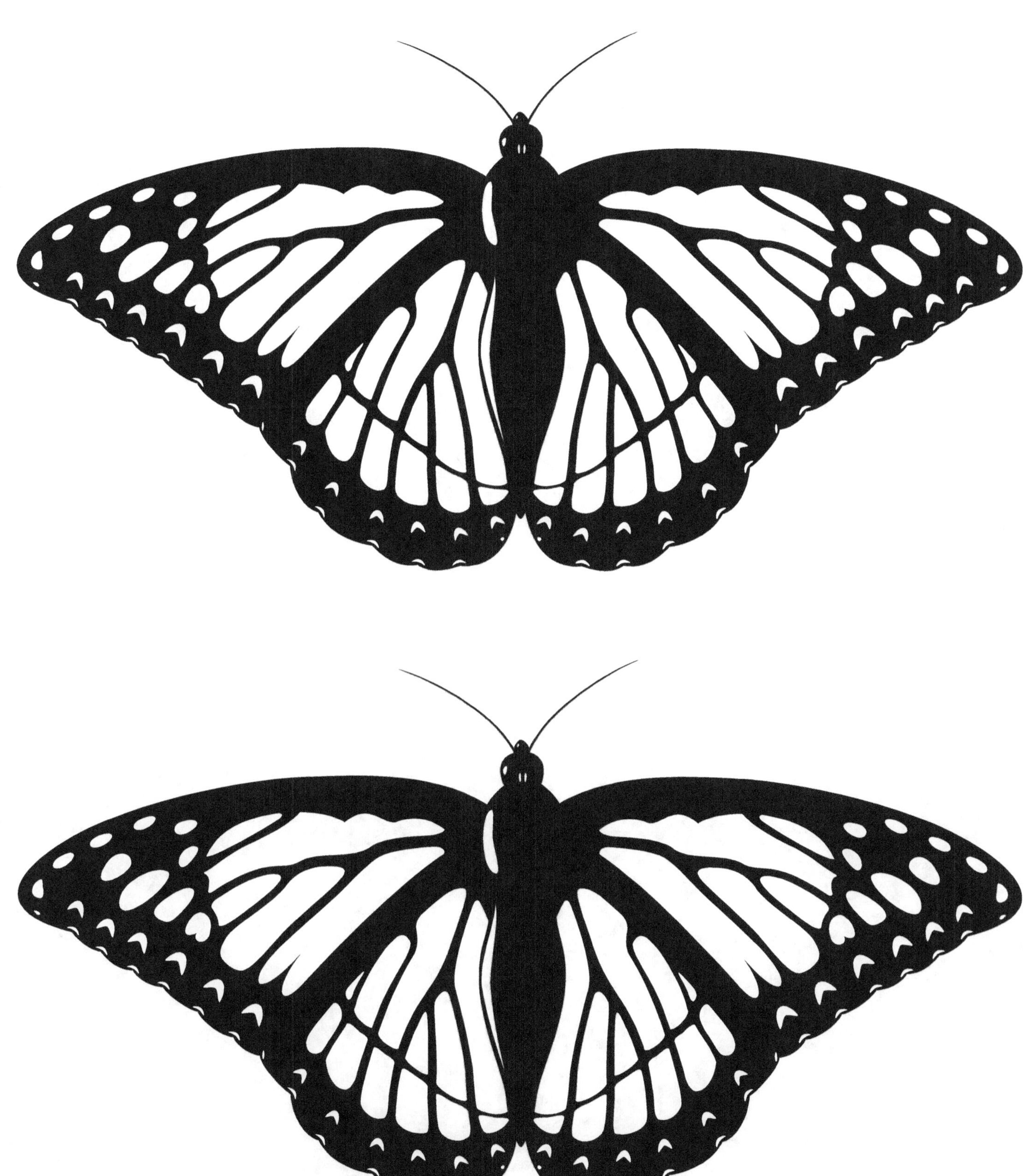

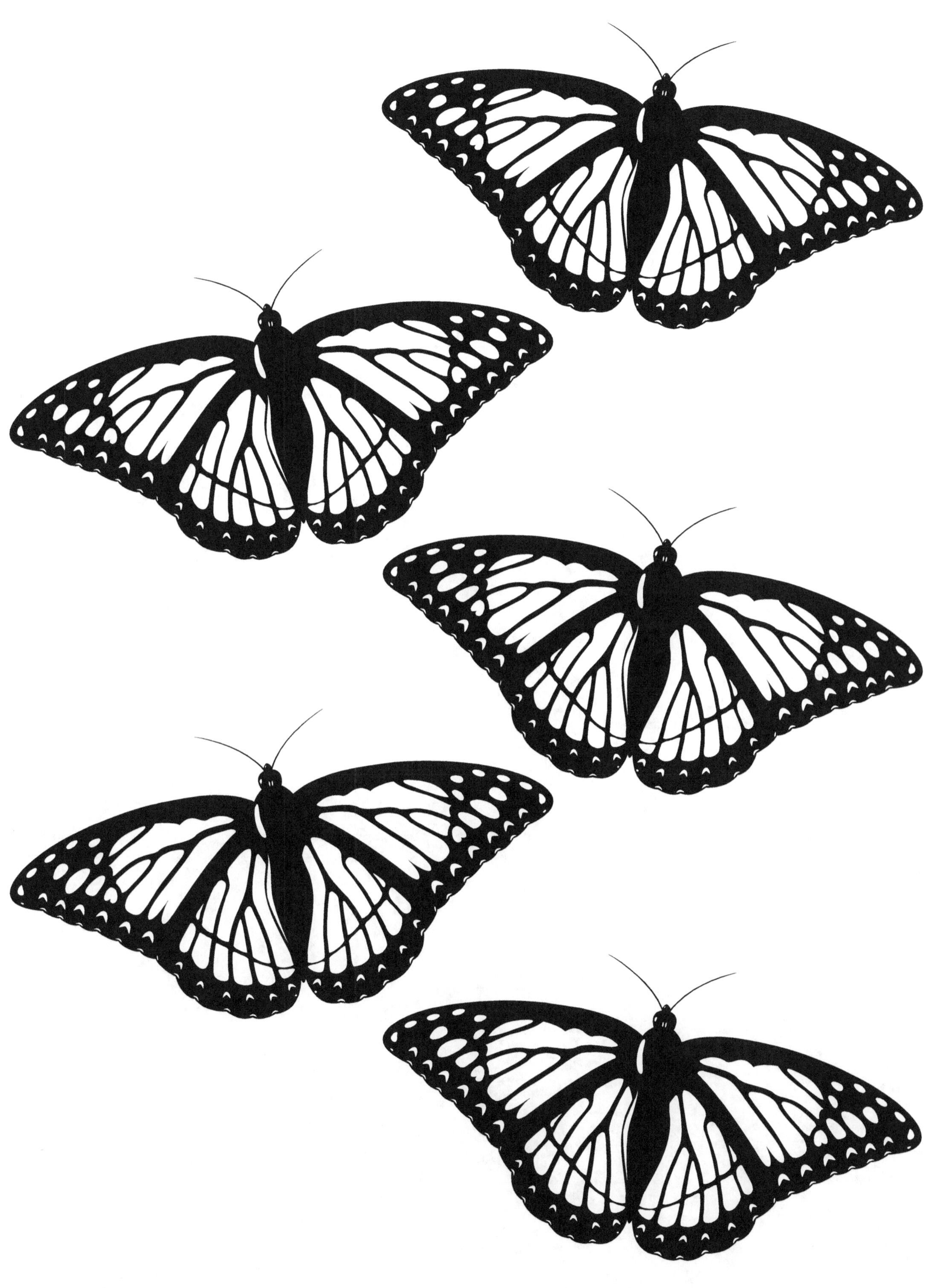

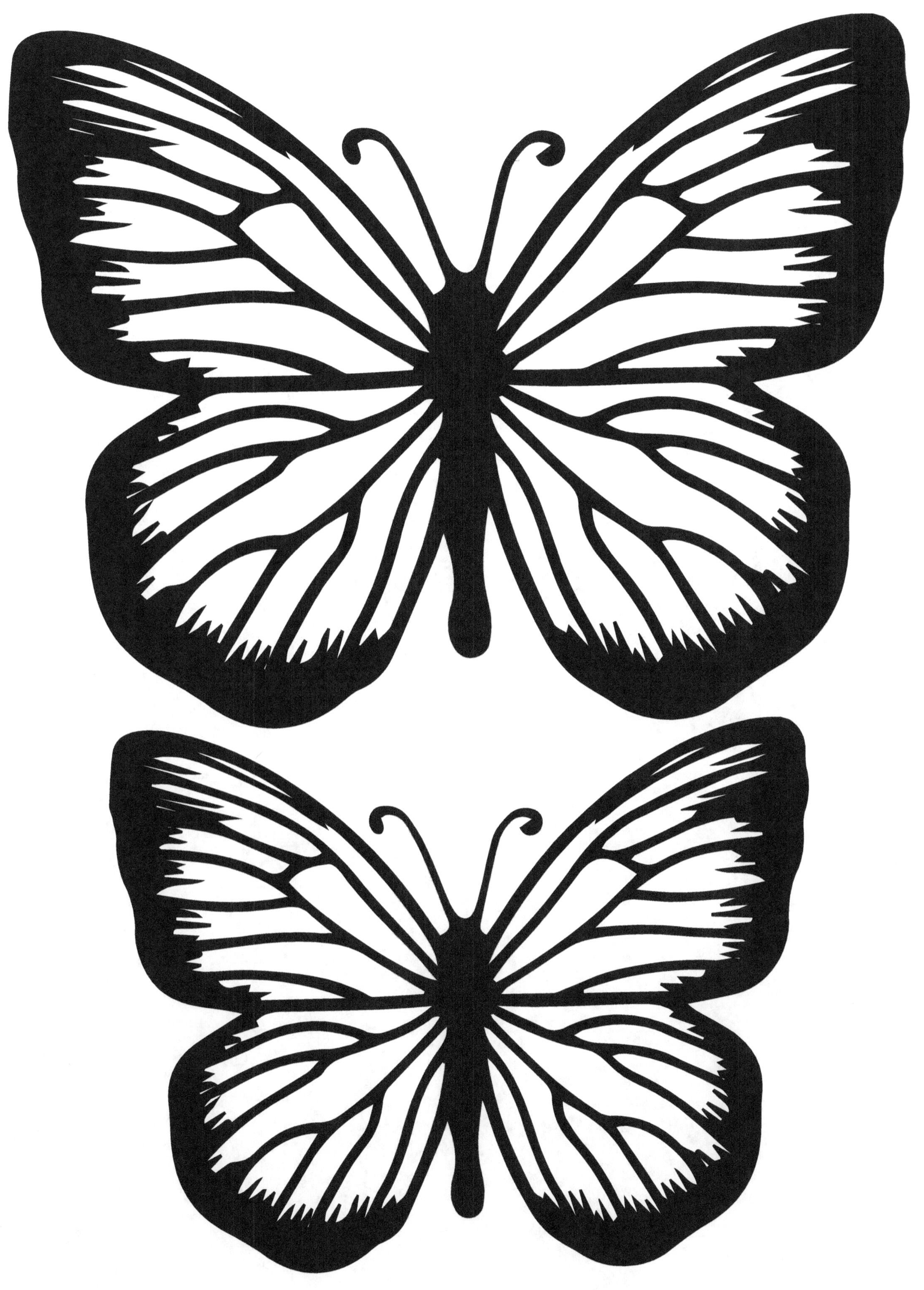

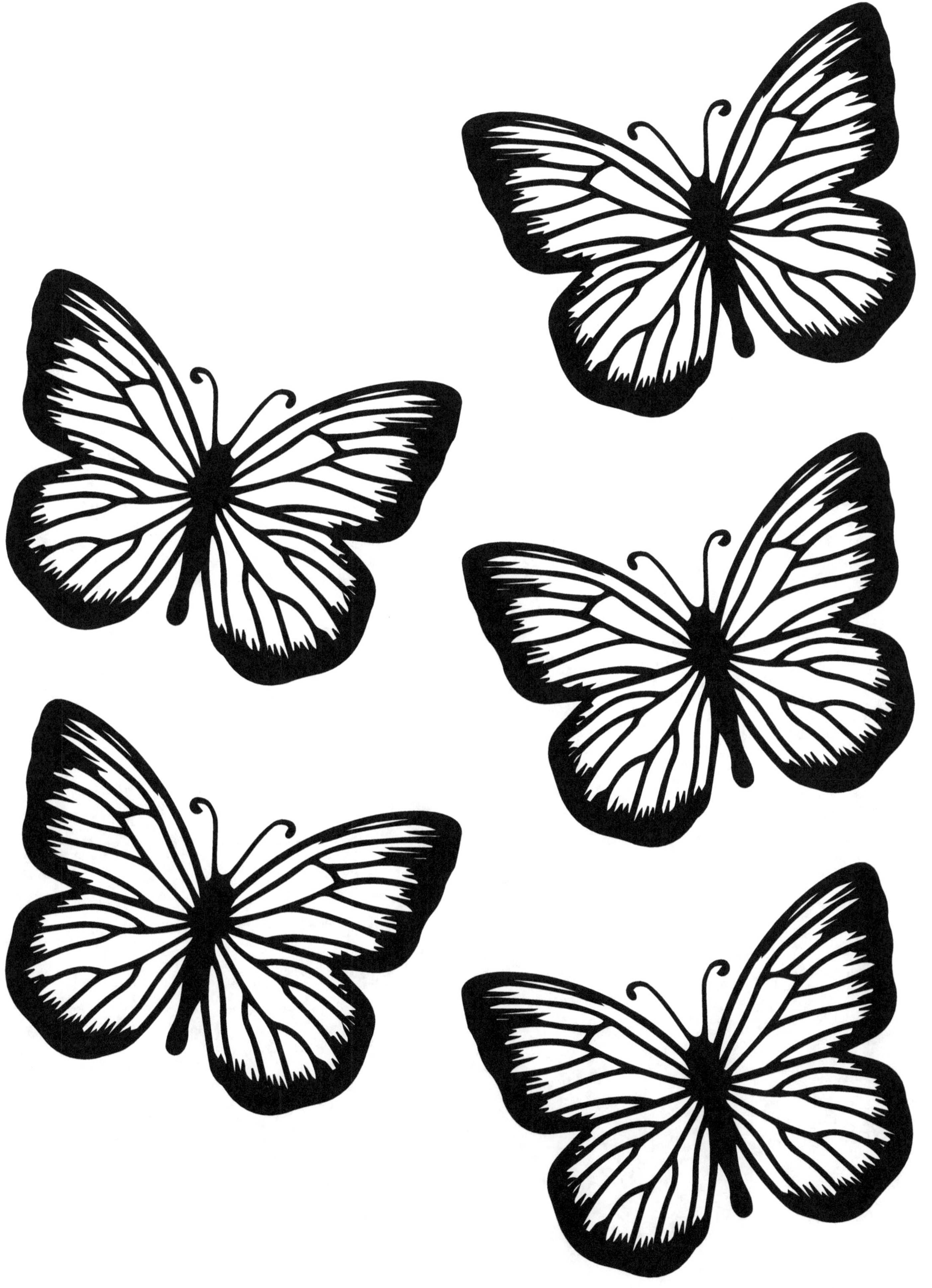

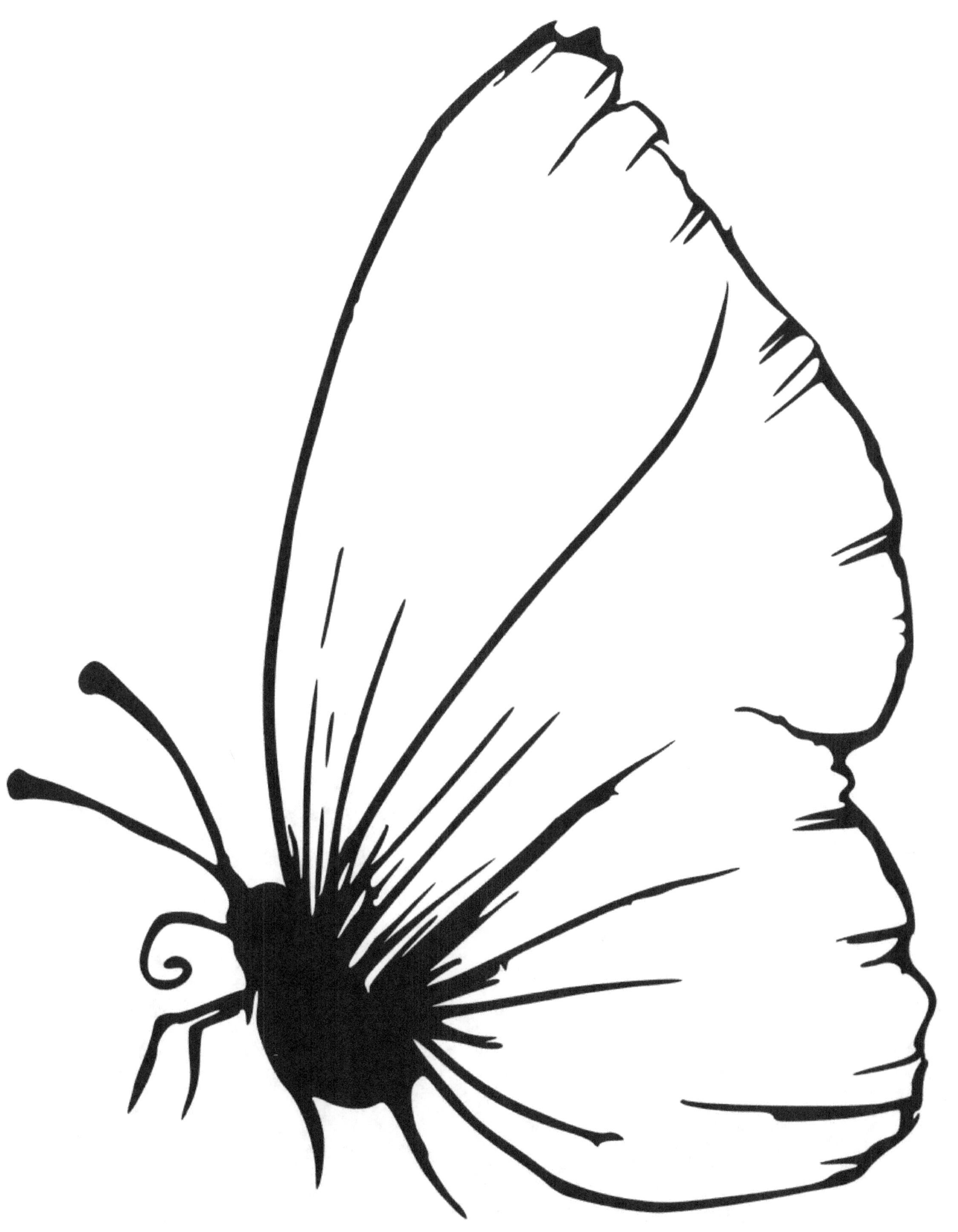

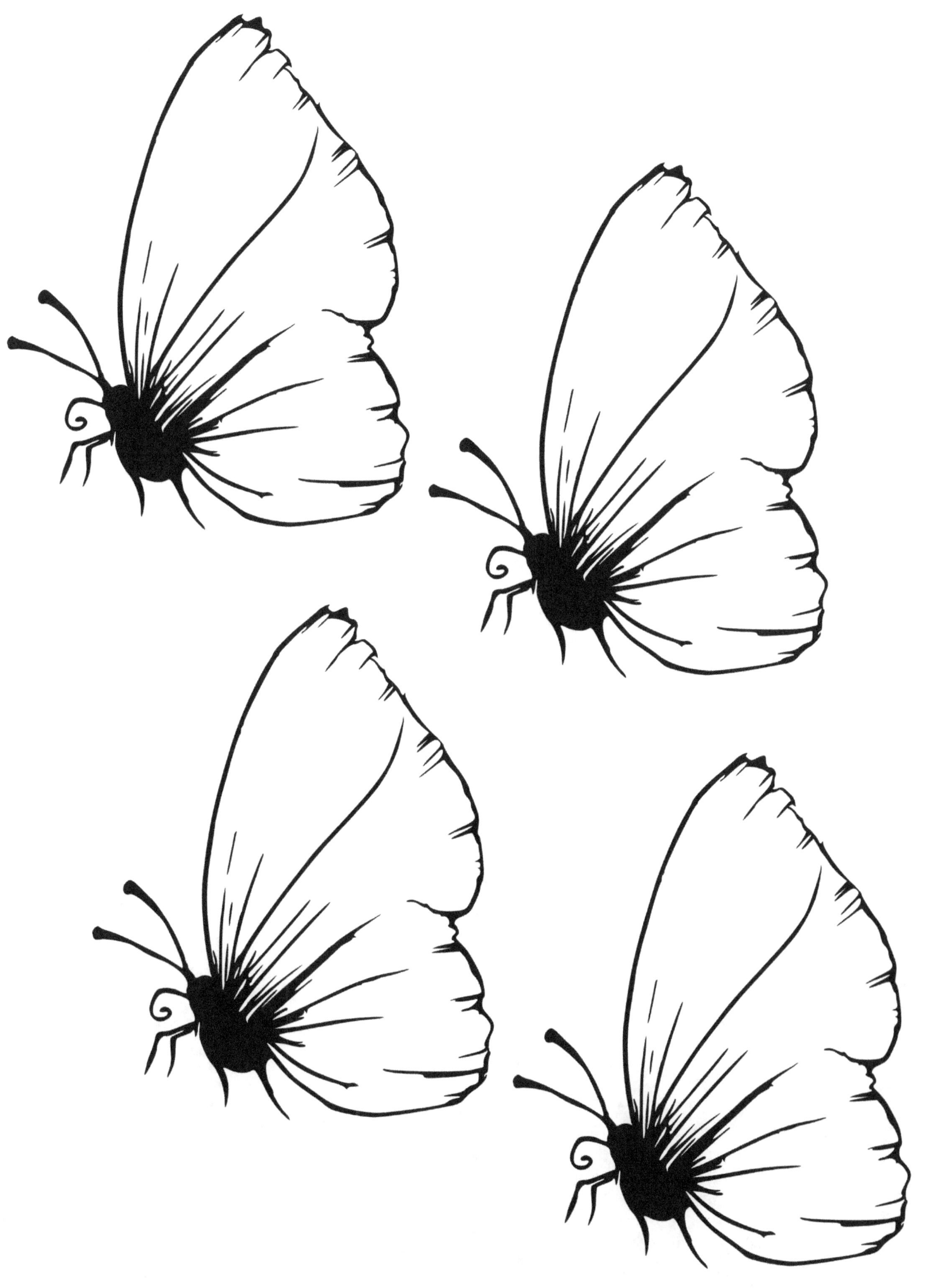

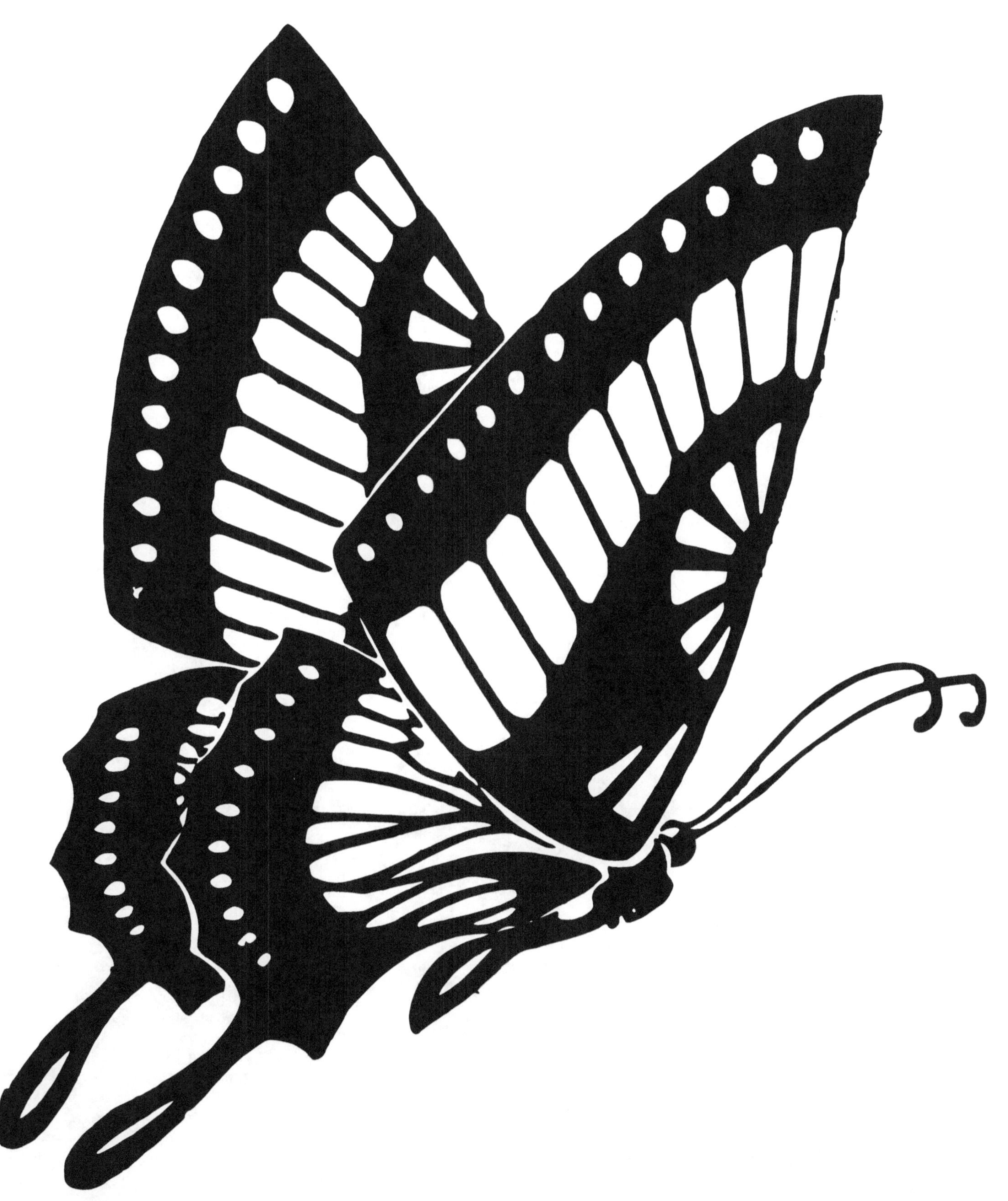

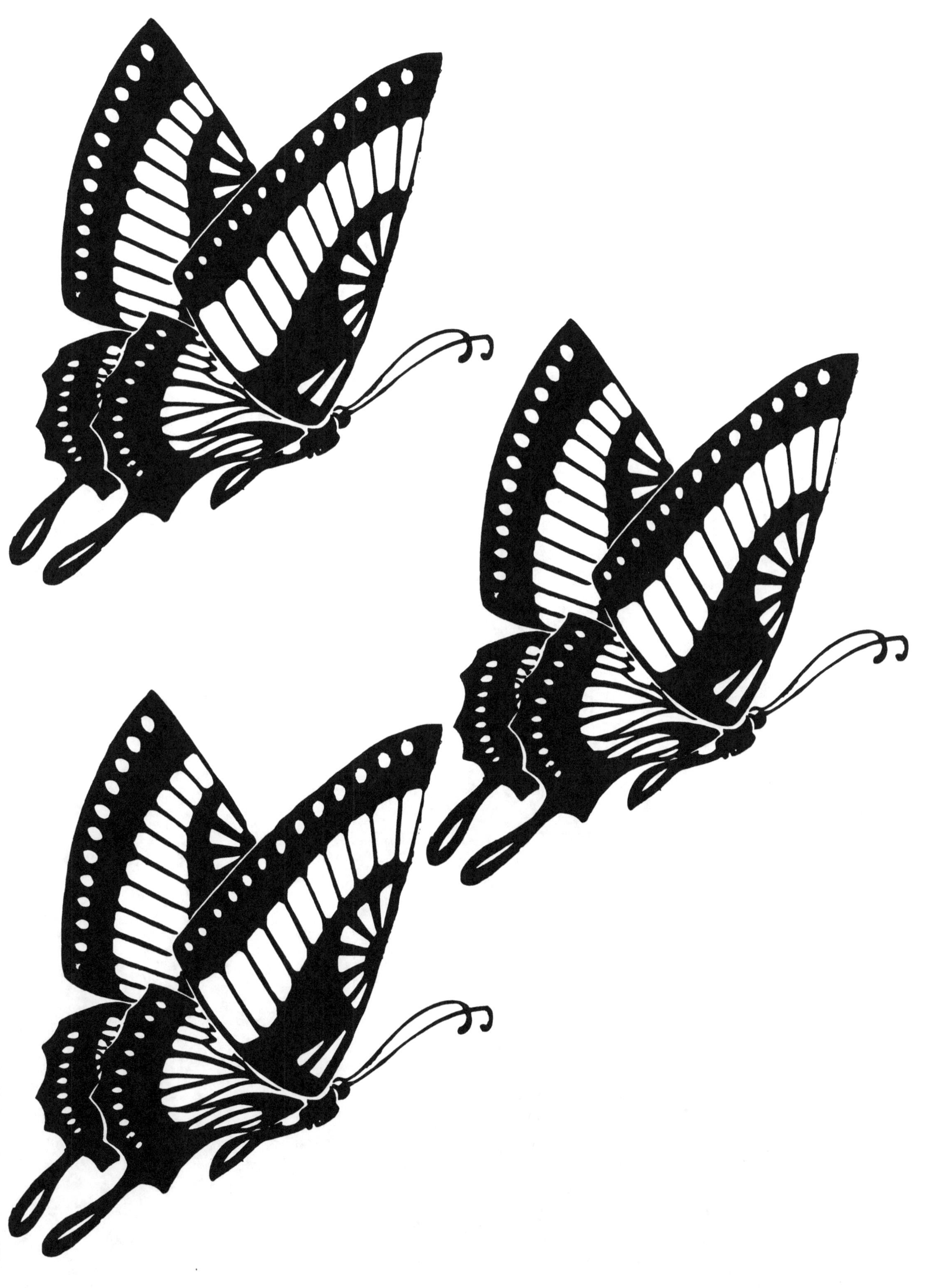

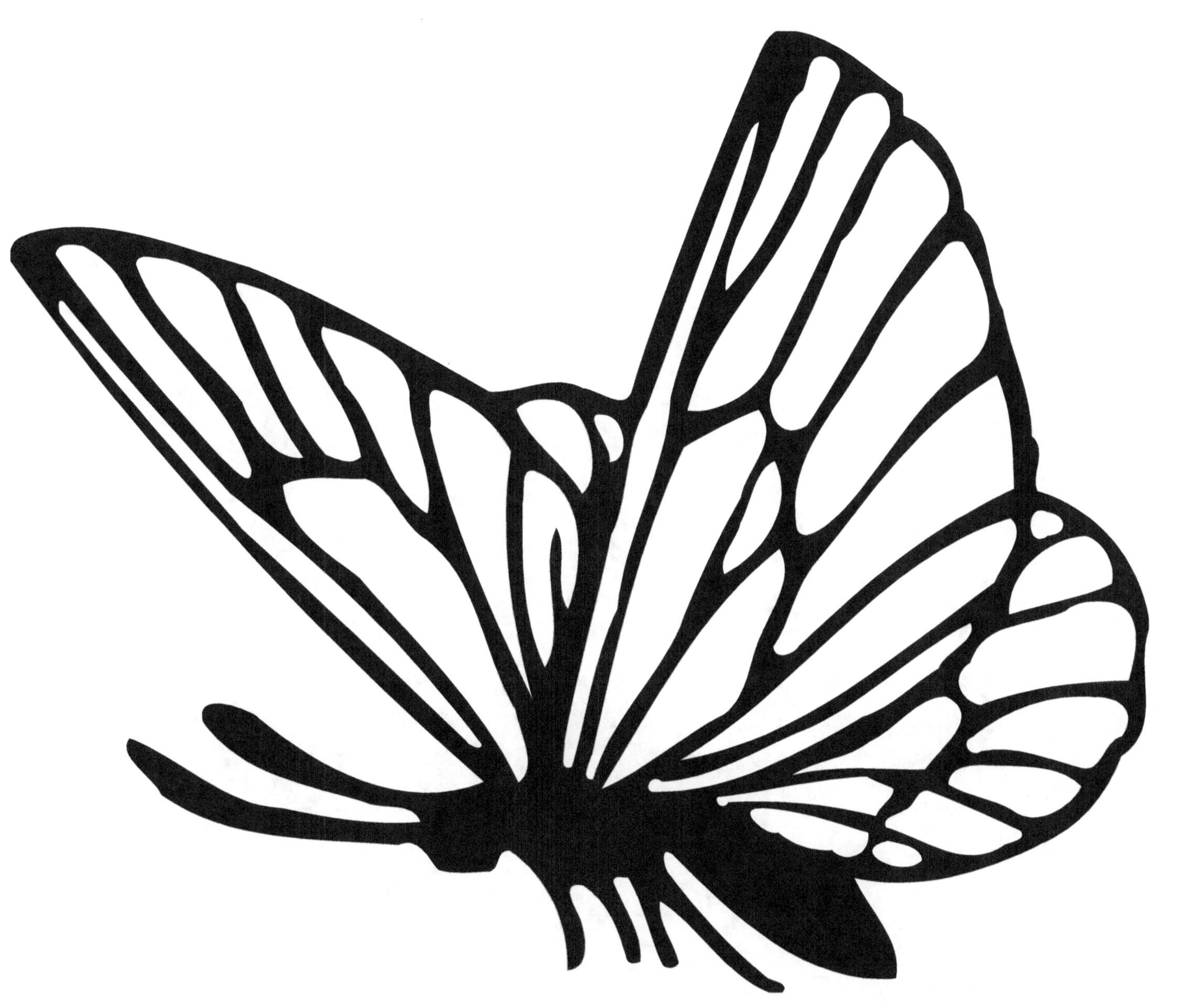

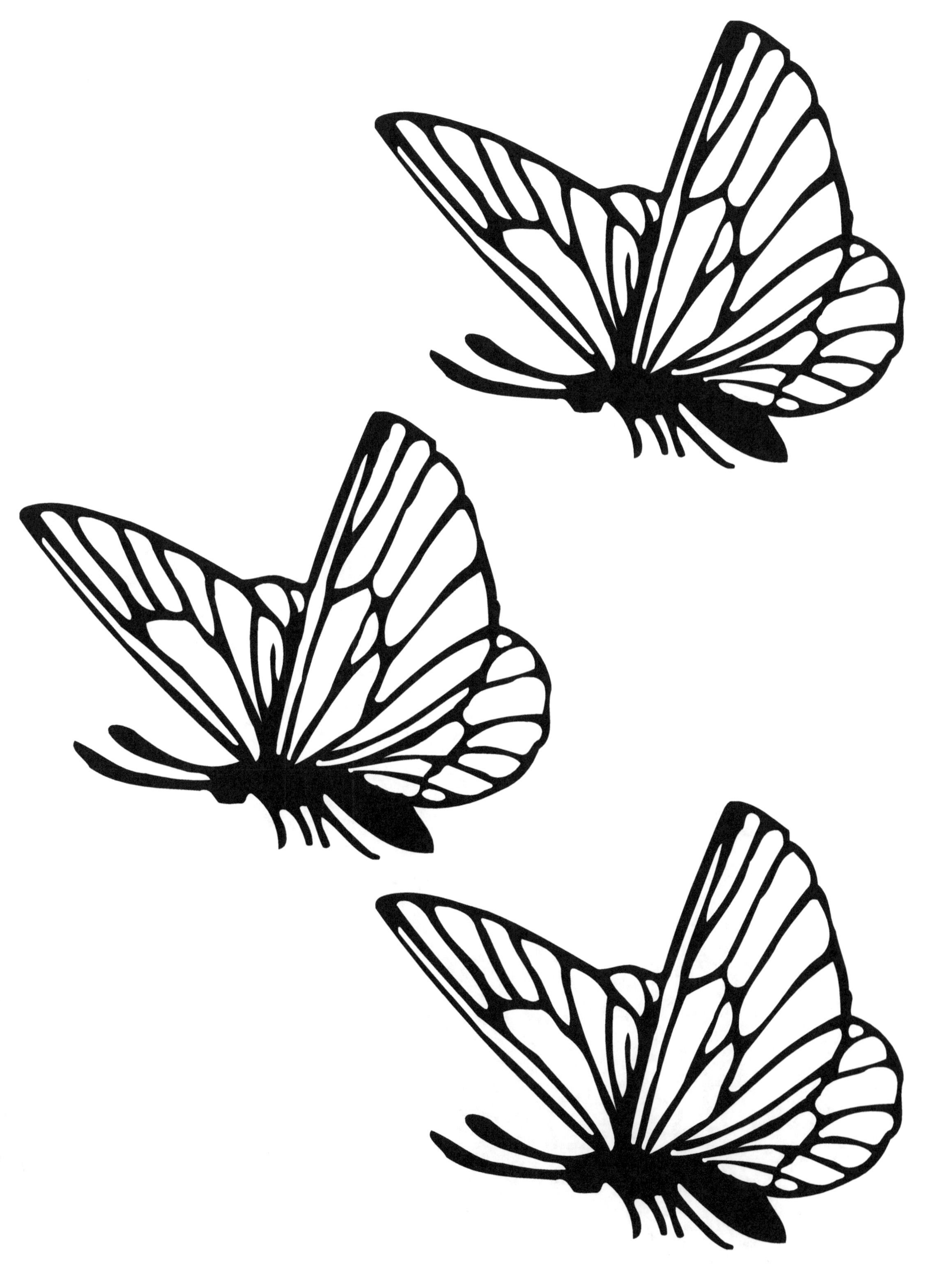